access to history

D1108609

STALIN AND KHRUSHCHEV: THE USSR, 1924–64

Second Edition

Alex M.

Michael Lynch

ashlee williams

803 4781

Hodder & Stoughton

A MEMBER OF THE HODDER HEADLINE GROUP

Acknowledgements

The front cover illustration shows a photograph of Joseph Stalin at the Yalta Conference in 1945, courtesy of Popperfoto.

The publishers would like to thank the following individuals, institutions and companies for permission to reproduce copyright illustrations in this book:
Corbis, page 17; David King Collection, pages 38, 64, 68, 90, 110; David Low, *Evening Standard*, 30ᵗʰ September 1938 © Solo Syndication/Centre for the Study of Cartoons and Caricature, University of Kent at Canterbury, page 88; Hulton-Deusch Collection/Corbis, page 8; London University (School of Slavonic and Eastern European Studies), page 113.

The publishers would like to also thank the following for permission to reproduce material in this book:
Cambridge University Press for an extract from *Stalinist Terror: New Perspectives* by J. Arch Getty and R. T. Manning, 1993; John Murray (Publishers) Ltd. for an extract from *Empire: The Russian Empire and its Rivals* by Dominic Lieven; Lawrence and Wishart for the extract from *Joseph Stalin: Collected Works*, London, 1955; Pearson Education Ltd., for the extract from *The Origins of the Cold War* by M. McCauley, 1983; PFD for the extract from *Eastern Approaches* by Sir Fitzroy MacLean, reprinted by permission of PFD on behalf of The Estate of Fitzroy MacLean; The Random House Group Limited for the extract from *The Dark Valley: A Panorama of the 1930s* by P. Brendon, published by Jonathan Cape.

Every effort has been made to trace and acknowledge ownership of copyright. The publishers will be glad to make suitable arrangements with any copyright holders whom it has not been possible to contact.

Orders: please contact Bookpoint Ltd, 130 Milton Park, Abingdon, Oxon OX14 4SB. Telephone: (44) 01235 827720, Fax: (44) 01235 400454. Lines are open from 9.00–6.00, Monday to Saturday, with a 24 hour message answering service. Email address: orders@bookpoint.co.uk

British Library Cataloguing in Publication Data
A catalogue record for this title is available from The British Library

ISBN 0 340 78144 0

First published 2001
Impression number   10 9 8 7 6 5 4 3
Year   2007 2006 2005 2004 2003 2002

Copyright © 2001 Michael Lynch

Typeset by Fakenham Photosetting Ltd, Fakenham, Norfolk.
Printed in Great Britain for Hodder & Stoughton Educational, a division of Hodder Headline Plc, 338 Euston Road, London NW1 3BH by Bath Press Ltd.

Contents

Preface

To the general reader

Although the *Access to History* series has been designed with the needs of students studying the subject at higher examination levels very much in mind, it also has a great deal to offer the general reader. The main body of the text (i.e. ignoring the 'Study Guides' at the ends of chapters) forms a readable and yet stimulating survey of a coherent topic as studied by historians. However, each author's aim has not merely been to provide a clear explanation of what happened in the past (to interest and inform): it has also been assumed that most readers wish to be stimulated into thinking further about the topic and to form opinions of their own about the significance of the events that are described and discussed (to be challenged). Thus, although no prior knowledge of the topic is expected on the reader's part, she or he is treated as an intelligent and thinking person throughout. The author tends to share ideas and possibilities with the reader, rather than passing on numbers of so-called 'historical truths'.

To the student reader

Although advantage has been taken of the publication of a second edition to ensure the results of recent research are reflected in the text, the main alteration from the first edition is the inclusion of new features, and the modification of existing ones, aimed at assisting you in your study of the topic at AS level, A level and Higher. Two features are designed to assist you during your first reading of a chapter. The *Points to Consider* section following each chapter title is intended to focus your attention on the main theme(s) of the chapter, and the issues box following most section headings alerts you to the question or questions to be dealt with in the section. The *Working on...* section at the end of each chapter suggests ways of gaining maximum benefit from the chapter.

There are many ways in which the series can be used by students studying History at a higher level. It will, therefore, be worthwhile thinking about your own study strategy before you start your work on this book. Obviously, your strategy will vary depending on the aim you have in mind, and the time for study that is available to you.

If, for example, you want to acquire a general overview of the topic in the shortest possible time, the following approach will probably be the most effective:

I   Read chapter I. As you do so, keep in mind the issues raised in the *Points to Consider* section.

2 Read the *Points to Consider* section at the beginning of chapter 2 and decide whether it is necessary for you to read this chapter.

3 If it is, read the chapter, stopping at each heading or sub-heading to note down the main points that have been made. Often, the best way of doing this is to answer the question(s) posed in the Key Issues boxes.

4 Repeat stage 2 (and stage 3 where appropriate) for all the other chapters.

If, however, your aim is to gain a thorough grasp of the topic, taking however much time is necessary to do so, you may benefit from carrying out the same procedure with each chapter, as follows:

1 Try to read the chapter in one sitting. As you do this, bear in mind any advice given in the *Points to Consider* section.

2 Study the flow diagram at the end of the chapter, ensuring that you understand the general 'shape' of what you have just read.

3 Read the *Working on …* section and decide what further work you need to do on the chapter. In particularly important sections of the book, this is likely to involve reading the chapter a second time and stopping at each heading and sub-heading to think about (and probably to write a summary of) what you have just read.

4 Attempt the *Source-based questions* section. It will sometimes be sufficient to think through your answers, but additional understanding will often be gained by forcing yourself to write them down.

When you have finished the main chapters of the book, study the 'Further Reading' section and decide what additional reading (if any) you will do on the topic.

This book has been designed to help make your studies both enjoyable and successful. If you can think of ways in which this could have been done more effectively, please contact us. In the meantime, we hope that you will gain greatly from your study of History.

Keith Randell & Robert Pearce

1 Introduction: The USSR, 1924–64

POINTS TO CONSIDER

This opening chapter provides a basic framework on which you can begin to build an understanding of Soviet history between 1924 and 1964. It has three main lines of approach. The first section briefly introduces the period and suggests why it is such an important one in world history. The second section introduces the two men who dominated these 40 years, Joseph Stalin and his successor Nikita Khrushchev. The final section defines the three basic issues that shaped Russian history in the period. a) How would power be exercised in the Soviet state, and by whom? b) How would the economy develop under Soviet Communism? c) What were to be the relations of the Soviet Union with the outside world? Even if you intend to be selective in the themes that you study, you are still advised to read all the parts of this opening section. This will help you gain a wider and more useful perspective.

KEY DATES

1924	Death of Lenin.
1924–29	Left *versus* Right power struggle.
1928	1st Five-Year Plan introduced.
1929	Trotsky defeated by Stalin.
	Beginning of collectivisation.
1932–33	Widespread Famine.
1933	2nd Five-Year Plan introduced.
1934	Beginning of purges.
1936–39	The Great Purges.
1938	3rd Five-Year Plan introduced.
1941–45	The Great Patriotic War.
1945	Beginning of Cold War.
1946	4th Five-Year Plan introduced.
1947	Leningrad purge.
1949	Soviet atom bomb detonated.
	5th Five-Year Plan introduced.
1953	Death of Stalin.
1953-56	Collective leadership.
1955	6th Five-Year Plan introduced.
1956	Khrushchev's 'Secret Speech' began de-Stalinisation process.
1956–64	Khrushchev led USSR.
1959	Seven-Year Plan introduced.
	Beginning of Sino-Soviet dispute.
1962	Cuban Missile crisis.
	Disastrous harvest.
1964	Khrushchev dismissed.

1 Background

> **KEY ISSUES** To what extent had the Russian Revolution been a rising of the masses?
> In what sense was Stalin the heir of Lenin?
> How did the failure of the Revolution to spread beyond the USSR affect developments within the USSR?

The Russian Revolution of 1917 was one of the most significant and controversial events of the twentieth century. According to those who made the revolution, what took place in Russia in 1917 was nothing less than the taking of power by the people, who then proceeded to create a new state and society in which the workers ruled. This interpretation asserted that Lenin, applying the revolutionary theories of Karl Marx, led the Bolshevik (Communist) Party to victory on behalf of the masses. During the next three years the Bolsheviks (the Reds) defended their revolution against the forces of reaction (the Whites) and fought off the invasions of Soviet Russia by hostile capitalist powers. By the time of Lenin's death in 1924, the triumphant Bolshevik Party had laid the basis for the development of the USSR as the world's first truly socialist state. Soviet Russia thus became the leader of – and the model for – all other nations and peoples who aspired to revolutionary change.

Essential to this Marxist analysis of what happened between 1917 and 1924 was the view that the Russian Revolution was a unique event in history. Marxists, holding that human history is determined by the class war, contended that 1917 marked the beginning of the world-wide rising of the proletariat (the exploited working class) against the bourgeoisie (the exploiting capitalist class).

Subsequent events made that view difficult to sustain. In the early 1990s the Communist Party (CPSU), after ruling the Soviet Union for 70 years, lost power. This was immediately followed by the break-up of the USSR. The collapse of Communism undermined the notion that 1917 had marked the start of an inevitable international Marxist revolution. The Russian Revolution began to be seen in a different light. Non-Marxists stressed how small-scale the October rising had been. They accepted that its consequences had been of great significance but they dismissed the interpretation of it as a mass movement. They described it, instead, as a Bolshevik coup, which succeeded not because the masses had supported it but because the Provisional Government against which it was directed was too weak to resist. Far from being a seizure of power *by* the masses, the October Revolution was a seizure of power *from* the masses. This was proved by the violent dispersal in January 1918 of the democratically-elected Constituent Assembly. The repression, which characterised the Bolsheviks' consolidation of their power, was to remain the outstanding feature of subsequent Soviet rule until its collapse in 1991.

Those who hold this view find support for it in the failure of revolution to spread elsewhere in Europe. It had been Lenin's belief that once the spark of revolution ignited in Russia the flame would spread across the neighbouring states. This did not happen. Brief glimmerings of revolution in Germany and Hungary were soon extinguished. When Bolshevik forces entered Poland in 1920, the Poles reacted not as revolutionary class brothers but as Polish patriots, and drove out the Red army which had come to 'liberate' them. Soviet Russia found itself the only revolutionary state in a hostile, capitalist world.

Between these two schools of thought – the one regarding the Revolution as a great liberating force, the other condemning it as a fundamentally oppressive movement – there has been a variety of interpretations, supportive, critical and neutral. That the Russian Revolution should continue to excite such interest among historians and political commentators shows how important the subject is held to be. The closing words of the *Communist Manifesto*, the equivalent of a Marxist bible, called on proletarian revolutionaries to fight for 'the forcible overthrow of all existing social conditions'. The Russian Bolsheviks took up this cry and appealed to the workers in all countries to rise against their governments. In 1919 the Bolsheviks created the Comintern (Communist International) for the specific purpose of organising revolution worldwide. The threat to the established order in Europe and elsewhere was very clear. The mutual fear and animosity that this created persisted throughout the period 1924–64.

The fierce debate about modern Russian history was not only between Marxists and non-Marxists. Continuously from the 1920s there were deep divisions among Communists themselves over the true nature of the Revolution after Lenin. The main divide was over Stalin. For some Communists, Stalin was the true heir to Lenin. For others, he was a usurper who had diverged from the true path laid by Lenin and in doing so betrayed the original 1917 Revolution.

2 Stalin and Khrushchev

> **KEY ISSUES** Did Stalin fulfil or betray the 1917 Revolution?
> Why did Khrushchev pursue a policy of de-Stalinisation?

Having manoeuvred himself into power by 1929, Stalin dominated the USSR for the next quarter of a century until his death in 1953. During that time he assumed heroic proportions in the eyes of the Soviet people. He presented himself to them as the successor of the great Lenin and became revered as the creator of a modern economy, the destroyer of the country's internal enemies, the warrior who led the nation to victory over fascism, and the leader who successfully guided his country into the nuclear age. Yet, only three years after his death, Stalin's god-like reputation began to be destroyed. His successor, Khrushchev, who led the USSR between 1956 and 1964, initiated a programme of 'de-Stalinisation'. This began in 1956 when Khrushchev made a series of startling revelations, listing the crimes that Stalin had perpetrated against the Communist Party. Khrushchev's main charge was that Stalin had corrupted the revolution by creating his own 'cult of personality'.

Khrushchev's attack on Stalin for his gross misuse of personal power did more than simply challenge the reputation of a past leader; it raised doubts about the record of the Soviet Union itself. How could a truly revolutionary state have allowed itself to be abused in this way? From that basic question arose a number of queries about the development of Soviet Communism after Lenin. The most insistent of these was whether Stalin had fulfilled or betrayed the Revolution begun by Lenin in 1917. The issue was of major importance. If the Bolshevik rising of 1917 had, indeed, been the first truly proletarian revolution, and if Lenin had been the founder of the first Marxist state, how was Stalin to be judged? Had Stalinism been a logical extension of the system established by Lenin or a perversion of it? Had Khrushchev's de-Stalinisation policy merely blackened Stalin's reputation or had it introduced real changes into the Soviet system? Such questions indicate some of the major issues with which historians concern themselves when studying the Soviet Union under Stalin and Khrushchev.

3 The Basic Problems for the USSR, 1924-64

> **KEY ISSUES** How was power to be exercised in the Soviet state? How would the economy develop under Soviet Communism? What were to be the relations of the Soviet Union with the outside world?

It was these three fundamental questions and the response of Stalin and Khrushchev to them that gave shape to the period 1924–64.

a) How was Power to be Exercised in the Soviet State?

In 1924 this issue was still undecided. Before they came to power in 1917, Lenin and the Bolsheviks had simply assumed that a successful proletarian revolution would lead to a withering away of the State. However, for most of the period 1917–24 they found themselves fighting for sheer survival. In consequence, the Bolsheviks became increasingly authoritarian. They outlawed their political rivals and greatly increased the size and scope of government. The question that Lenin left in 1924 was whether this absolutism would be maintained. Would the Soviet Union return to establishing the freedoms that had inspired many of the revolutionaries of 1917 or would it continue its drift towards totalitarianism, a system of authority imposed from above in which the masses had no say?

b) How would the Economy Develop Under Soviet Communism?

When the Bolsheviks took over the Russian economy in 1917, their intention had been to transform it from a capitalist to a socialist system. Lenin directed that a start be made towards bringing industry under State control as a first stage in the centralisation of the economy. This was possible with industry, but agriculture proved a different matter. The war against Germany and Austria (1914–17), the Revolution in 1917, and the Civil War (1918–20) had disrupted food production and distribution to the point where Russia was starving. In 1921, in an effort to prevent famine, Lenin introduced the New Economic Policy (NEP). This was a concession to the peasants which allowed them to keep their surplus produce and sell it at a profit. Lenin readily admitted that this was a return to capitalist methods, but he argued that the move was justified by the desperate circumstances.

The NEP worked in the short term; the peasants responded by producing more food for the nation. The question that Lenin left to his successors was how long should the NEP be continued. A serious division in Party thinking occurred over this. There were those, known as the Left Bolsheviks, who wanted the abandonment of the NEP since they regarded it as being contrary to true socialism. They were opposed by the Right Bolsheviks, who considered that it should be maintained for as long as it continued to provide food. How would Stalin respond to this issue? How would he interpret the Soviet Union's agricultural and industrial needs, and by what methods would he attempt to satisfy them?

c) What were to be the Relations of the Soviet Union with the Outside World?

For the Bolsheviks, this had been more than simply a question of foreign policy. In accordance with their Marxist beliefs, they had expected their seizure of power in Russia to be quickly followed by world revolution. But since this had not happened, what should Soviet Russia's policy be in a world that resolutely refused to copy the Bolshevik model? Should the Soviet Union still commit itself to the cause of international revolution or should it settle for its own internal consolidation and national development? That was the problem Lenin's successors had to address in their conduct of Soviet foreign policy.

Working on Chapter I

You should concentrate on gaining a basic understanding of the key points in each of the three sections of this chapter. Although the period 1917–24 lies outside the scope of this book, and you may not be studying the Russian Revolution itself, you will have difficulty in understanding Stalin and Khrushchev if you do not have a grasp of what happened in those earlier seven years. This does not need to be detailed knowledge but you do need to appreciate what had occurred in Russia between 1917 and 1924. Reference to the Introduction and Conclusion of *Reaction and Revolutions: Russia 1881–1924*, the companion volume to this book, would help you to achieve this.

At this early stage there may be some terms and ideas that are new to you. Try not to let this confuse you. You will find that if you go about your work systematically, building up your knowledge section by section and chapter by chapter, your understanding will keep pace with the demands placed upon it. Section 3 sets out three basic questions which underlay the whole period. The full significance of these will emerge as you work through the book. The Conclusion will return to these questions and re-examine them in the light of what you have studied in all the other chapters.

2 Stalin's Rise to Power

POINTS TO CONSIDER

When Lenin died in 1924 he left no obvious successor. Few Russian Communists gave thought to Stalin as a likely leader. Yet five years later, after a bitter power struggle, it was Stalin who had outmanoeuvred his rivals and established his authority over the party and the nation. How he achieved this is the subject of this chapter. You need to grasp who Stalin's opponents were and what views they represented. The material requires close attention as some of the twists and turns in the story are quite complex. The first two sections provide important background material, describing Stalin's character and personality and outlining the role he had played as a revolutionary before 1924. The remaining sections analyse Stalin's defeat of his chief personal rival, Leon Trotsky, and of his two main sets of opponents, the Left Bolsheviks and the Right Bolsheviks

KEY DATES

1924 Death of Lenin,
Politburo declared USSR to be ruled by a collective leadership.
1925 Trotsky lost his position as War Commissar,
Kamenev and Zinoviev headed 'the New Opposition'.
1926 Trotsky joined Kamenev and Zinoviev in Left political bloc, which was defeated by Stalin's supporters.
1927 Stalin persuaded Congress to expel Trotsky from the CPSU.
1928 Stalin attacked the Right (led by Tomsky, Bukharin and Rykov) over agricultural policy.
1929 The leading figures on the Right finally defeated by Stalin and demoted in the CPSU;
Trotsky exiled from the USSR.

1 The Roots of Stalin's Power

> **KEY ISSUE** How had Stalin been able to rise up the Bolshevik ranks?

Hindsight tells us that, however much Lenin may have wished to prevent Stalin from succeeding him as leader, the basis of Stalin's power had been laid even before Lenin's death. The Party had, unintentionally, already provided Stalin with the means of assuming control. To understand how this had happened we need to

-Profile-

1879	Born in Georgia
1899	His revolutionary activities led to expulsion from Tiflis seminary
1905	Met Lenin for first time
1912	Adopted the name Stalin Became a member of the Central Committee of the Bolshevik Party Helped to found *Pravda*
1914–17	In exile in Siberia
1917	Returned to Petrograd People's Commissar for Nationalities
1919	Liaison Officer between Politburo and Orgburo (1919) Head of the Workers' and Peasants' Inspectorate (1919)
1922	General Secretary of the Communist (Bolshevik) Party
1924	Delivered the oration at Lenin's funeral

Stalin, meaning 'man of steel', was not his real name. It was simply the last in a series of aliases that Joseph Vissarionovich Djugashvili adopted in order to avoid detection as a revolutionary. Before 1917, Stalin spent a large part of his life in hiding and in exile. This has left many gaps in the story of his younger days. Nevertheless, the main features can be identified. He was born in 1879 in Georgia, a rugged province in the south of the Russian Empire, renowned for the fierceness of its people. Blood feuds and family vendettas were common. Georgia had only recently been incorporated into the Russian Empire. Tsarist government officials often wrote in exasperation of the difficulties of trying to control a savage people who refused to accept their subordination to Russia.

This was the stock from which Stalin came. His drunken father eked out a miserable existence as a cobbler and the family appears to have lived in constant poverty. There have been suggestions that both Stalin's admiration of things Russian and his contempt for middle-class intellectuals derived from a sense of resentment over his humble Georgian origins. As is common in unsophisticated societies, the Georgians were markedly religious. Stalin's mother was a particularly devout woman and it was largely through her influence that her son was enrolled as a student, training for the priesthood in a Georgian-Orthodox seminary in Tbilisi (Tiflis). This did not denote religious fervour on Stalin's part. The fact was that at this time in imperial Russia attendance at a church academy was the only way to obtain a

Russian-style education, an essential requirement for anyone from the provinces who had ambition. Stalin seems to have been no more than competent as a student; in any case, he was attracted less by theology than by the political ideas with which he came into contact.

In the seminary records for 1899 there is an entry beside Stalin's name that reads 'expelled for not attending lessons – reasons unknown'. We now know the reasons; he had become involved in the Georgian resistance movement, agitating against tsarist control. His anti-government activities drew him into the Social Democratic Workers' Party. This was the Marxist party that in 1903 split into two opposed groups: the Mensheviks, led by Plekhanov, and the Bolsheviks, led by Lenin. From the time of his expulsion from the seminary to the Revolution of 1917 Stalin was a committed follower of Lenin. He threw himself into the task of raising funds for the Bolsheviks; his specialities were bank hold-ups and train robberies. To the authorities he was just another Georgian bandit. By 1917 he had been arrested eight times and had been sentenced to various periods of imprisonment and exile. These privations served only to toughen his already hardened character. Afterwards he tended to despise those revolutionaries who had escaped such experiences by fleeing to the relative comfort of self-imposed exile abroad.

Stalin spent the war years, 1914–17, in exile in Siberia. He returned to Petrograd in March 1917 under the amnesty for political prisoners that followed the February Revolution. He had played a part in neither the war nor the February Revolution, but his efforts in the Bolshevik cause had already brought him to Lenin's notice. Before 1917 the Bolshevik Party had been only a few thousand strong and Lenin had known the great majority of members personally. He had been impressed by Stalin's organising ability and willingness to obey orders. He once described him as 'that wonderful Georgian', a reference to his work as an agitator among the non-Russian peoples. Lenin showed his favour by having Stalin promoted. By 1912 Stalin had risen to become one of the six members of the Central Committee, the policy making body of the Bolshevik Party. He had also helped to found the Party's newspaper, *Pravda* (Russian for 'Truth').

Stalin's role in the October Revolution is difficult to disentangle. Official accounts, written after he had taken power, were a mixture of distortion and invention, with any unflattering episodes totally omitted. What is reasonably certain is that Stalin was loyal to Lenin after the latter's return to Petrograd in April 1917. Lenin instructed the Bolsheviks to abandon all co-operation with other parties and to devote themselves to preparing for a seizure of power. As a Leninist, Stalin was opposed to the 'October deserters', such as Kamenev and Zinoviev, who advised against a Bolshevik coup until the Party was stronger. Later, in the post-Lenin power struggle, he would use the record of their lack of resolution in October 1917 as a weapon against them.

During the period of crisis and civil war that accompanied the efforts of the Bolsheviks to consolidate their authority after 1917, Stalin's non-Russian background proved invaluable. His knowledge of the minority peoples of the old Russian Empire led to his being appointed Commissar (Minister) for Nationalities. In that role he became the Bolshevik organiser for the whole of the Caucasus region during the Civil War from 1918 to 1921. The position entitled him to exercise military authority, and this led to a number of disputes with Trotsky, the Bolshevik Commissar for War. Superficially the quarrels were about strategy and tactics, but at a deeper level they were a clash of wills. They proved to be the beginning of a deep personal rivalry between Stalin and Trotsky.

Ironically, it was as Commissar for Nationalities that Stalin, the 'wonderful Georgian', first aroused Lenin's distrust. Despite his earlier commitment to the independence of Georgia, Stalin was off-hand and dismissive towards its national spokesmen, and Lenin was obliged to intervene personally to resolve the situation. Lenin had further cause to complain when he learned from his wife, Krupskaya, that Stalin had treated her discourteously. Lenin expressed his anger in a written statement that became known as 'Lenin's Testament'. In this Lenin warned that Stalin, since becoming General Secretary of the Party in 1922, had concentrated too much power in his hands. He went on to propose that Stalin be removed from his position. But this was not done. Lenin was too incapacitated during the last year of his life to be politically active. At his death in January 1924, he had still not taken any formal steps to remove Stalin, and the 'Testament' had not been made public.

appreciate the nature of Soviet government as it had developed after 1917.

When Lenin and the Bolsheviks took power in the October Revolution they were untrained in the skills of government. All their efforts had been directed towards preparing for revolution. They had not planned a detailed programme for governing Russia and had to learn the job as they went along. Governments in most countries could call upon tradition and precedent to guide them. A revolutionary government had no such guide-lines; the procedures to be followed were uncertain. This created opportunities for individual advancement which, in more stable times, would not have existed. It is arguable that in a traditional system of government, with a clearly defined pattern of promotion, Stalin would have made little progress. His attempts to rise would have been obvious and, therefore, preventable.

However, Soviet Russia in 1924 was not a traditional system of government. Lenin had given no clear indication what the power-structure should be after him. In the uncertain atmosphere that followed his death, a number of pieces of luck helped Stalin promote his own claims; it was very much a matter of being in the right place at the right time. However, it would be wrong to ascribe his success wholly to good fortune. The luck had to be used. Stalin may have lacked brilliance, but he did not lack ability. His particular qualities of dogged perseverance and willingness to undertake laborious administrative work were ideally suited to the times.

The government of Soviet Russia, as it had developed by 1924, had two main features: the Council of Peoples' Commissars (equivalent to a cabinet of ministers), responsible for creating government policies, and the Secretariat (equivalent to the civil service), responsible for carrying out those policies. Both these bodies were staffed and controlled by the Bolshevik Party. It has to be stressed that the vital characteristic of this governmental system was that the Party ruled. By 1922 all other political parties had been outlawed and Soviet Russia was a one-party state. Membership of that one party was essential for all who held administrative or government posts at whatever level.

Council of Peoples' Commissars – the executive

|

the Secretariat – the administrative system

|

both serving and controlled by the Bolshevik Party

The Soviet government was thus the formal expression of the Party's control. In this situation the various conferences, committees and congresses that made up the organisation of Party and government became increasingly important. As government grew in scope certain posts, which initially had not been considered especially significant, began to provide their holders with the levers of power. This had not been the intention, but was the unforeseen result of the emerging pattern of Bolshevik rule. It was in this context that Stalin's previous appointments to key posts in both government and Party proved vital. These had been:

People's Commissar for Nationalities (1917)
Liaison Officer between Politburo and Orgburo (1919)
Head of the Workers' and Peasants' Inspectorate (1919)
General Secretary of the Communist (Bolshevik) Party (1922)

As Commissar for Nationalities Stalin was in charge of the officials in the many regions and republics that made up the USSR (the official title of the Soviet state after 1922). As the officer responsible for liaison between the Politburo (the Central Committee's inner cabinet) and the Orgburo (the Party's Bureau of Organisation), Stalin was in a unique position to monitor both the Party's policy and its personnel. As Head of the Workers' Inspectorate, he was entitled to oversee the work of all government departments. As General Secretary, he recorded and conveyed Party policy. Most important of all, he used his position to build up personal files on all the members of the Party. Nothing of note happened they he did not know about.

These posts had not been meant to confer power on Stalin. The Politburo, to which he had belonged since 1917, had appointed him simply because of his reputation for hard work. Indeed, it was about this time that an exiled Menshevik described him as 'a grey blur', and Trotsky referred to him as 'an eminent mediocrity'. Even when he was made General Secretary of the Party there was little excitement. Nobody appeared to see it as a portent. Some of his biographers suggest that Stalin himself did not at first realise the full importance of what had happened. Writers such as Edward Crankshaw and Norman Stone argue that Stalin was not a planner who carefully plotted his way to the top but an opportunist who, because of his willingness to seize the moment, found power coming within his grasp. Whatever Stalin's intentions may have been at this stage, it would appear that few of his contemporaries had grasped just how powerful the holding of these positions had made him.

Stalin became the indispensable link in the chain of Communist Party and Soviet government command. Above all, what these posts gave him was the power of patronage, the right to appoint individuals to official posts in the Party and government. He used this authority to place his own supporters in key positions. Since they then owed their place to him (he could fire as well as hire), Stalin could count on their support in the voting in the various committees and congresses which made up the organisation of the Soviet Union.

Such were the levers in Stalin's possession during the Party in-fighting over the succession to Lenin. No other contender came anywhere near matching Stalin in his hold on the Party machine. Whatever the ability of the individuals or groups who opposed him or the strength of their arguments, he could always out-vote and out-manoeuvre them.

Stalin's advantages over his rivals had been increased by certain recent changes in the structure of the Communist Party. Between 1923 and 1925 the Party had undertaken 'the Lenin enrolment' with the aim of increasing the number of true proletarians in its ranks. This resulted in the CPSU membership rising from 340,000 in 1922 to 600,000 by 1925. The new members were predominantly poorly educated and politically unsophisticated, but they were fully aware that the many privileges which came with Party membership depended on their being loyal to those who had first admitted them into the Bolshevik ranks. The responsibility for supervising and vetting 'the Lenin enrolment' had fallen largely to the officials in the Secretariat who worked directly under Stalin as General Secretary. In this way, the expansion of the Party added to his growing power of patronage. E.H. Carr described this as being a change 'from the elite party of Lenin to the mass party of Stalin'. It provided the General Secretary with a reliable body of votes in the various Party committees at local and central level.

Another lasting feature of Lenin's period that proved of great value to Stalin was what had become known as the 'attack upon factionalism'. This referred to Lenin's condemnation of the Party's squabbling during the Civil War period. What this rejection of 'factionalism' effectively did was to frustrate any serious attempt to criticise Party decisions or policies. Contrary to the tradition of internal debate among Bolsheviks, it became extremely difficult to mount any form of legitimate opposition within the CPSU. Stalin benefited directly from the ban on criticism of the Party line. The charge of 'factionalism' provided him with a ready weapon for resisting challenges to the authority he had begun to exercise.

There was an accompanying factor that legitimised Stalin's position. Stalin became heir to what has been described as the 'Lenin legacy'. By this is meant the tradition of authority and leadership that Lenin had established during his lifetime, and the veneration in which he was held after his death. It is barely an exaggeration to say that in the eyes of the Communist Party Lenin became a god; his words, actions and decisions became unchallengeable, and all arguments and disputes within the Party were settled by reference to his statements and writings. Lenin became the measure of the correctness of Soviet theory and practice. Soviet Communism became Leninism. After 1924, if a Party member could assume the mantle of Lenin and appear to carry on Lenin's work, he would establish a formidable claim to power. This is what Stalin began to do.

Here a paradox needs to be explained. In theory the Bolshevik Party was a collective organisation. In accordance with its Marxist principles, it was suspicious of leaders and individuals. It believed that it had the right to wield authority because it represented the will, not of any individual but of the proletarian masses. The Party had never elected a leader and not even Lenin had been accorded that title formally. However, no matter what the theory may have been, the practice proved to be very different. The very intensity of the Bolsheviks' struggle for survival after 1917 meant that power shifted increasingly to the centre. Such had been Lenin's moral ascendancy among the Bolsheviks that he had come to represent the Party itself. The collective principle had in practice been superseded by the leadership principle. It is arguable that this was a return to the Russian tradition of central authority that the tsars had exercised.

2 The Power Struggle: Stalin versus Trotsky

> **KEY ISSUES** What lay at the root of the rivalry between Stalin and Trotsky? Why was Trotsky unable to mount a successful challenge to Stalin? What were the essential differences between 'Socialism in One Country' and 'Permanent Revolution' as responses to Soviet Russia's needs in the 1920s?

After Lenin's death the Politburo (consisting of Rykov, Tomsky, Kamenev, Zinoviev, Trotsky and Stalin) publicly proclaimed their intention to continue as a collective leadership, but behind the scenes the competition for individual authority had already begun. In the manoeuvring, Stalin gained an advantage by being the one to deliver the oration at Lenin's funeral. Appearances mattered, and the sight of Stalin as leading mourner suggested a continuity between him and Lenin, an impression heightened by the contents of his speech in which, in the name of the Party, he humbly dedicated himself to follow in the tradition of the departed leader:

1   In leaving us, comrade Lenin commended us to hold high and pure the great calling of Party Member. We swear to thee, Comrade Lenin, to honour thy command.
    In leaving us, Comrade Lenin commanded us to keep the unity of our
5 Party. We swear to thee, Comrade Lenin, to honour thy command. In leaving us, Comrade Lenin ordered us to maintain and strengthen the dictatorship of the proletariat. We swear to thee, Comrade Lenin, to exert our full strength in honouring thy command.
    In leaving us, Comrade Lenin ordered us to strengthen with all our
10 might the union of workers and peasants. We swear to thee, Comrade Lenin, to honour thy command. In leaving us, Comrade Lenin ordered us to strengthen and expand the Union of the Republics. We swear to thee, Comrade Lenin, to honour thy command.
    In leaving us, Comrade Lenin enjoined us to be faithful to the

15 Communist International. We swear to thee, Comrade Lenin, that we shall dedicate our lives to the enlargement and reinforcement of the union of the workers of the whole world, the Communist International.[1]

Trotsky was conspicuous by his absence from the funeral. This was one of a series of tactical mistakes that Stalin's chief rival made. Trotsky later complained that Stalin had not informed him of the date of the funeral. This may well have been true, but it seemed a very lame excuse and raised doubts about his respect for Lenin's memory. Trotsky had a complex personality. He was one of those figures in history who may be described as having been their own worst enemy. Despite his many gifts and his intellectual brilliance, he had serious weaknesses that undermined his chances of success. At times, he was unreasonably self-assured; at other critical times, he suffered from diffidence and lack of judgement. An example of this had occurred earlier, at the time of Stalin's mishandling of the Georgian question. Lenin's annoyance with Stalin had offered Trotsky a golden opportunity for undermining Stalin's position, but for some reason Trotsky had declined to attack. A possible clue to his reluctance is that he felt inhibited by his Jewishness. Trotsky knew that, in a society of deeply ingrained anti-Semitism, his race made him an outsider. A remarkable example of his awareness of this occurred in 1917, when Lenin offered him the post of Deputy Chairman of the Soviet government. Trotsky rejected it on the grounds that his appointment would be an embarrassment to Lenin and the government. 'It would', he said, 'give enemies grounds for claiming that the country was ruled by a Jew'. It may be that similar reasoning in January 1924 allowed Stalin to gain an advantage over him.

The remarkable feature of all this is that Trotsky, by his own account, was very conscious of the danger that Stalin represented. In 1924 he prophesied to Smirnov, one of his own supporters, that Stalin would become 'the dictator of the USSR'. When Smirnov expressed surprise, Trotsky gave a strikingly accurate analysis of the basis of Stalin's power in the Party:

1 He is needed by all of them; by the tired radicals, by the bureaucrats, by the Nepmen, the upstarts, by all the worms that are crawling out of the upturned soil of the manured revolution. He knows how to meet them on their own ground, he speaks their language and he knows how 5 to lead them. He has the deserved reputation of an old revolutionary. He has will and daring. Right now he is organising around himself the sneaks of the Party, the artful dodgers.[2]

At this juncture an obvious hurdle in Stalin's way was Lenin's 'Testament'. If it were to be published it would discredit his claim to have been Lenin's loyal lieutenant. However, here, as so often during this period, fortune favoured him. Had the document been made public, not only would the criticisms of Stalin have been revealed, but also those concerning Trotsky, Zinoviev and Kamenev. Nearly all the members of the Politburo had reason for suppressing the 'Testament'. This is evident from its contents:

1 **25 December 1922**
   Since he became General Secretary, Comrade Stalin has concentrated in his hands immeasurable power, and I am not sure that he will always know how to use that power with sufficient caution. On the other hand
5 Comrade Trotsky, as has been shown already by his struggle against the Central Committee over the question of the People's Commissariat of Means of Communication, is distinguished not only by his outstanding qualities (personally he is the most capable man in the present Central Committee) but also by his excess of self-confidence and a readiness to
10 be carried away by the purely administrative side of affairs.
   The qualities of these two outstanding leaders of the present Central Committee might lead quite accidentally to a split, and if our Party does not take steps to prevent it the split might arise unexpectedly. I shall not try to describe any other members of the Central Committee
15 according to their personal qualities. I will simply remind you that the October episode involving Zinoviev and Kamenev [who had tried to dissuade the Bolsheviks from rising at that point] was not, of course, accidental but that it ought not to be used seriously against them, any more than the non-Bolshevism of Trotsky.
20   Of the younger members of the Central Committee I would like to say a few words about Bukharin. Bukharin is not only the most valuable and the most able theorist in the Party but may legitimately be considered the favourite of the whole Party. But his theoretical views can only with the greatest hesitation be regarded as fully Marxist.

1 **Postscript, 4 January 1923**
   Stalin is too rude, and this fault, entirely supportable in relations amongst us Communists, becomes insupportable in the office of General Secretary. Therefore, I propose to the comrades to find a way
5 of removing Stalin from that position and to appoint another man who in all respects differs from Stalin only in superiority; namely, more patient, more loyal, more polite, less capricious, and more attentive to comrades.[3]

When the Central Committee were presented with this document in May 1924, they realised that it was too damning broadly to be used exclusively against any one individual. They agreed to its being shelved indefinitely. Trotsky, for obvious personal reasons, went along with the decision, but in doing so he was declining yet another opportunity to challenge Stalin's right to power. In fact it was Trotsky, not Stalin, whom the Politburo regarded as the greater danger. Kamenev and Zinoviev joined Stalin in an unofficial triumvirate within the Politburo. Their aim was to isolate Trotsky by exploiting his unpopularity with large sections of the Party. The 'Lenin enrolment' helped them in this. The new proletarian members were hardly the type of men to be impressed by the cultured Trotsky. The seemingly down-to-earth Stalin was much more to their liking.

		-Profile-
1879	born into a Ukrainian Jewish family	
1898	convicted of revolutionary activities and exiled to Siberia	
1902	adopted the name Trotsky, escaped from exile and joined Lenin in London	
1903	sided with the Mensheviks in the SD split	
1905	became Chairman of St. Petersburg Soviet	
1906	exiled again	
1907	escaped again and fled abroad	

1917   returned to Petrograd after February Revolution, was the principal organiser of the October coup, appointed Foreign Affairs Commissar

1918   negotiated the Treaty of Brest-Litovsk

1918-20 as War Commissar, created the Red Army

1921   crushed the Kronstadt Rising
         destroyed the trade unions in Russia

1924–27 outmanoeuvred in the power struggle with Stalin

1927   sentenced to internal exile

1929   banished from USSR

1929–40 lived in various countries
         wrote prodigiously on revolutionary theory, in opposition to Stalin

1940   assassinated in Mexico on Stalin's orders

Trotsky's real name was Leon (Lev) Bronstein. He was born into a Jewish landowning family in the Ukraine in 1879. Rebellious from an early age, he sided with the peasants on his family's estate. Yet, like Lenin, he rejected 'economism', the attempt to raise the standards of peasants and workers by improving their conditions. He wanted to intensify class warfare by exploiting grievances, not to lessen it by introducing reforms.

As a revolutionary, Trotsky's sympathies lay with the Mensheviks and it was as a Menshevik that he became president of the St. Petersburg Soviet during the 1905 Revolution. His activities led to his arrest and exile. Between 1906 and 1917 he lived in a variety of foreign countries, developing his theory of 'permanent revolution', the notion that revolution was not a single event but a continuous process of international class warfare. Following the collapse of tsardom in the February Revolution, Trotsky returned to Petrograd and immediately joined the Bolshevik Party. He became chairman of the Petrograd Soviet, a position which he used to organise the Bolshevik rising which overthrew the Provisional Government in October 1917.

In the Bolshevik government that then took over, Trotsky became Commissar for Foreign Affairs. He was the chief negotiator in the Russo-German talks that resulted in Russia's withdrawal from the war in 1918 under the Treaty of Brest-Litovsk. He then became Commissar for War, and achieved what was arguably the greatest success of his career, the victory of the Red Army in the Civil War of 1918-20. As a hard liner, Trotsky fully supported Lenin's repressive policy of war communism. He plotted the destruction of the Russian trade unions, and in 1921 ordered the suppression of the rebellious Kronstadt workers.

In terms of ability, Trotsky ought to have been the main contender in the power struggle that followed Lenin's death. But he was never fully accepted by his fellow Bolsheviks, which enabled Stalin to isolate him. Trotsky's concept of permanent revolution was condemned as anti-Soviet, since it appeared to put the pursuit of international revolution before the establishment of 'socialism in one country', Stalin's term for the consolidation of Communist rule in the USSR. In 1929 Trotsky was exiled from the USSR. He spent his last 11 years in a variety of countries, attempting to develop an international following opposed to the Soviet regime. In 1939 he founded the Fourth International, a movement of anti-Stalin Marxists drawn from some 30 countries. Trotsky's end came in 1940 in Mexico City, when a Soviet agent acting on Stalin's direct orders, killed him by driving an ice-pick into his head.

Believers are still to be found who regard Trotsky as the Bolshevik with the human touch, the man who would have led the Russian Revolution towards democratic socialism. But this interpretation is hard to sustain in the face of the record of his fanatical behaviour as a Soviet commissar between 1917 and 1921. In the 1990s, Dmitri Volkogonov, the Russian biographer of Lenin, Stalin and Trotsky, produced evidence from previously unexamined Russian state papers to show that Lenin and Trotsky had worked together on a deliberate policy of terror that precisely foreshadowed the later Stalinist tyranny. Trotsky's enforced militarisation of labour, his crushing of the trade unions, the extreme severity he used to discipline the Red Army, his savagery against the Kronstadt rebels in 1921, and his ferocity towards the Russian peasantry undermine the romantic image of him as 'the angel of enlightenment' in an otherwise cruel world. In justification of his terror tactics, Trotsky wrote:

1 Violent revolution was necessary because the undeferrable demands of history proved incapable of clearing a road through the apparatus of parliamentary democracy. Anyone who renounces terrorism in principle must also renounce the political
5 rule of the working class. The extensive recourse, in the Civil War, to execution by shooting is to be explained by this one simple but decisive fact. Intimidation is a powerful instrument of both foreign and domestic policy. The revolution kills individuals and thus intimidates thousands.[4]

The attitude of Party members towards Trotsky is an important part of any explanation of Stalin's success and Trotsky's failure. Because Trotsky was flamboyant and brilliant, while Stalin was unspectacular and methodical, colleagues tended to regard the former as dangerously ambitious and the latter as reliably self-effacing. Trotsky was the type of person who attracted either admiration or suspicion, but seldom loyalty. That was why he lacked a genuine following. It is true that he was highly regarded by the Red Army, whose creator he had been, but this was never matched by any comparable political support in the Party. This resulted in Trotsky's invariably appearing to be an outsider. Adding to his difficulties in this regard was the doubt about his commitment to Bolshevism. Until 1917, as Lenin had noted in his 'Testament', Trotsky had been a Menshevik. This led to the suspicion that his conversion had been a matter of expediency rather than conviction. Many of the old-guard Bolsheviks regarded Trotsky as a Menshevik turncoat.

Such views were to dog him when, having overcome his initial loss of nerve, he tried to take the attack to his opponents in the mid-1920s. Trotsky bitterly condemned the growth of bureaucracy in the Party and appealed for a return to 'Party democracy'. He pressed his views in the annual Party Congresses and in the meetings of the Central Committee and the Politburo. He expanded his arguments in a series of essays, the most controversial of which was *Lessons of October*, in which he criticised Kamenev and Zinoviev for their past disagreements with Lenin. The assault was ill-judged, since it invited retaliation in kind. Trotsky's Menshevik past and his divergence from Leninism were highlighted in a number of books and pamphlets, most notably Kamenev's *Lenin or Trotsky*.

Stalin could stand back and observe his rivals destroying each other. Bearing in mind his later extremism (see page 70), it is an extraordinary fact that at this time Stalin was able to play the role of the great moderate who refused to become embroiled in Party warfare. Even Trotsky's censures on bureaucracy, which were obviously aimed principally at him, left Stalin largely unscathed. What Trotsky meant by bureaucracy was the abandonment of genuine discussion within the Party and the growth in the centralised power of the Secretariat, which was able to make decisions and operate policies without reference to ordinary Party members. Trotsky complained that officials were becoming the masters, rather than the servants, of the Party.

In trying to expose Stalin's bureaucratic tendencies, Trotsky overlooked the essential fact that Bolshevik rule since 1917 had always been a bureaucracy. It might have been called other names, like Secretariat and *apparat*, and its officials might have been known by good revolutionary terms like *cadres*, but it was a bureaucracy all the same. So, in attacking it, Trotsky was going against what Lenin had sanctioned and Stalin had continued. After all, it was because the Soviet state functioned as a bureaucracy that Party members received privileges in political and public life. Trotsky's anti-bureaucratic line was hardly likely to gain significant support from party members who had a vested interest in bureaucracy.

With Trotsky worsted in the dispute and forced temporarily to retreat, Stalin was free to take the initiative. His open attack on Trotsky and other rivals centred on two fundamental issues in the politics of the Soviet Union after 1924. These were the NEP and 'Socialism in one Country'. The issues overlap but it makes for clarity if they are considered separately.

a) NEP

The New Economic Policy went back to 1921. At the Party Congress of that year Lenin, faced by the famine that was decimating large parts of Russia, had persuaded his fellow Bolsheviks to accept the NEP. Essentially, this was a relaxation of the severe economic controls (known as War Communism) enforced by the government during the Civil War. Under the NEP the peasants were allowed to sell their surplus produce for profit, traditional markets were permitted, and the restrictions on the use of money were lifted. These concessions were a relaxing of strict socialism. Lenin admitted this but said, 'let the peasants have their little bit of capitalism as long as we retain the power'. Lenin had visualised the NEP as a temporary measure but, since it fulfilled its chief objective of providing enough food for the Russian population, it was retained as the official Bolshevik policy towards the peasantry.

At the time of Lenin's death the question was already being asked as to whether the NEP was to last indefinitely. The Party members who were unhappy with it saw its retention as a betrayal of revolutionary principle. They objected to the preferential treatment of the peasantry which the Policy entailed. The peasants, they argued, were being allowed to slow the pace of Soviet Russia's advance to a truly proletarian state, which had been the whole object of the 1917 Revolution. Critics of the NEP were broadly referred to as Left Communists, while those supported it were known as Right Communists.

It is important not to exaggerate the difference of principle between Left and Right. Although fierce disputes were to arise over the issue, initially the disagreement was simply about timing: how long should the NEP be allowed to run? However, in the power struggle of the 1920s these superficial differences deepened into questions of political orthodoxy and Party loyalty. A rival's attitude towards the NEP might be a weakness to be exploited; if it could be established that his views indicated deviant Marxist thinking it became possible to undermine his position in the Party.

b) Socialism in One Country

Closely related to the NEP debate was the question of how the Soviet Union should plan for the future. This would have been a demanding issue regardless of whether there had been a power struggle. What the rivalry for leadership did was to intensify the argument. The USSR was a poor country. If it was to modernise and overcome its poverty it would have to industrialise. All recent history had shown that a strong industrial base was an absolute essential for a modern state and there was little disagreement among Soviet Communists about that. The quarrel was not over whether the USSR should industrialise, but over how and at what speed.

At the time of the October Revolution, Russia had a predominantly agricultural economy. 80 per cent of the population were peasants. The irony was that the proletarian revolution had occurred in a country without a proletariat. It was very difficult to make October 1917 fit the classic Marxist model of a workers' revolution. Lenin had been very conscious of this and had decided that the link between the Party and the peasants must be maintained for the foreseeable future. The industrial expansion that had taken place in the previous century, in such countries as Germany and Britain, had relied on a ready supply of exploitable natural and human resources, and the availability of capital for investment. Russia was rich in natural resources, but these had yet to be effectively exploited, and it certainly did not possess large amounts of capital. Nor could it easily borrow any; after 1917 Bolshevik ideology explicitly rejected capitalist methods of finance. Moreover, even if the Bolsheviks had been willing to ignore their Marxist theory by borrowing, there were few countries after 1917 prepared to risk the dangers of investing in revolutionary Russia.

The only usable resource, therefore, was the Russian people themselves. If the Soviet Union was to industrialise it would have to be done by persuading or forcing the peasant population to produce a food surplus which could then be sold abroad to raise capital for industrial investment. Both Left and Right agreed that this was the only solution, but, whereas the Right were content to rely on persuasion, the Left demanded that the peasantry be coerced into line.

It was Trotsky who most clearly represented the view of the Left on this. However, for him the industrialisation debate was secondary to the far more demanding question of Soviet Russia's role as the organiser of international revolution. What inspired Trotsky's politics was his belief in 'permanent revolution'. He interpreted the events in Russia since 1917 simply as a prelude to proletarian revolution worldwide. If it came to a choice, the interests of the USSR would have to be subordinated to the greater cause of international revolution, which he regarded not as a single event but as a continuous (permanent) process in which risings took place from country to country.

Trotsky asserted that true revolutionary socialism could be achieved in the USSR only if an international uprising took place. The Soviet Union, he believed, could not stand alone. With its vast peasant population and undeveloped proletariat, Russia would prove 'incapable of holding her own against conservative Europe'. He contended that the immediate task of the CPSU was not to concern itself with the internal needs of the Soviet Union but 'to export revolution'. This was very much the voice of the international Mensheviks, Trotsky's old party. Once again he had cast doubt on the genuineness of his Bolshevism.

Stalin countered Trotsky's notion of 'permanent revolution' with his own concept of 'Socialism in one country'. He meant by this that the USSR's first task was to overcome its present agricultural and industrial problems by its own unaided efforts, and then go on to build a modern state, the equal of any nation in the world. Under this banner, Stalin was able to characterise Trotsky as an enemy of the Soviet Union. Trotsky's ideas were condemned as an affront to Lenin and the Bolshevik Revolution. An image was created of Trotsky as an isolated figure, a posturing Jewish intellectual, whose abstractions about international revolution threatened the security of the Soviet Union.

Trotsky's position was further weakened by the fact that throughout the 1920s the Soviet Union had a constant fear of invasion by the combined capitalist nations. Although this fear was ill-founded, the tense atmosphere it created made Trotsky's notion of the USSR's engaging in foreign revolutionary wars appear even more irresponsible. A number of historians, including E.H. Carr and Isaac Deutscher, have remarked on Stalin's ability to rally support and silence opponents at critical moments by taking on the role of the great Russian patriot intent on saving the nation from its internal and external enemies.

3 The Defeat of Trotsky and the Left

> **KEY ISSUE** What were the basic weaknesses of the 'New
> Opposition' in their challenge to Stalin?

Trotsky's failure in the propaganda war of the 1920s meant that he
was in no position to persuade either the Politburo or the Central
Committee to vote for his proposals. Stalin's ability 'to deliver the
votes' in the crucial divisions was decisive. Following a vote against
him in the 1925 Party Congress, Trotsky was relieved of his position as
Commissar for War. Kamenev and Zinoviev, the respective Chairmen
of the Moscow and Leningrad Soviets, played a key part in this. They
used their influence over the local Party organisations to ensure that
it was a pro-Stalin, anti-Trotsky, Congress that gathered.

Kamenev and Zinoviev had been motivated by a personal dislike of
Trotsky, who had sought to embarrass them by reminding the Party of
their failure to support Lenin in 1917. Now it was their turn to be
ousted. With Trotsky weakened, Stalin turned to the problem of how
to deal with these two key figures, who were now his potential rivals.
In the event, they created a trap for themselves. In 1925 Kamenev and
Zinoviev, worried by the USSR's economic backwardness, publicly
stated that it would require the victory of proletarian revolution in the
capitalist nations in order for the Soviet Union to achieve socialism.
Zinoviev wrote: 'When the time comes for the revolution in other
countries and the proletariat comes to our aid, then we shall again go
over to the offensive. For the time being we have only a little breath-
ing space'. He called for an end to the NEP, for restrictions on the
peasants, and enforced industrialisation.

It was understandable that Kamenev and Zinoviev, party bosses in
the Soviet Union's only genuinely industrial areas, Moscow and
Leningrad, should have thought in these terms. Their viewpoint
formed the basis of what was termed the 'New (or United)
Opposition' but it appeared to be indistinguishable from Trotskyism.
It was no surprise, therefore, when Trotsky joined his former oppo-
nents in 1926 to form a 'Trotskyite-Kamenevite-Zinovievite' opposition bloc. Again, Stalin's control of the Party machine proved critical.
The Party Congress declined to be influenced by pressure from the
'New Opposition'. Stalin's supporters among the Right Communists
(chiefly Bukharin, Rykov and Tomsky) combined to outvote the bloc.
Kamenev and Zinoviev were dismissed from their posts as Soviet
Chairmen, to be replaced by two of Stalin's staunchest allies, Molotov
in Moscow and Kirov in Leningrad. Soon afterwards, Trotsky was
expelled from both the Politburo and the Central Committee.

Trotsky still did not admit defeat. In 1927, on the tenth anniversary
of the Bolshevik rising, he tried to rally support in a direct challenge
to Stalin's authority. Even fewer members of Congress than before

were prepared to side with him and he was again outvoted. His complete failure led the Congress to accept Stalin's proposal that Trotsky be expelled from the Party altogether. An internal exile order against him in 1927 was followed two years later by his total exile from the USSR.

Stalin's victory over Trotsky was not primarily a matter of ability or principle. Stalin won because Trotsky lacked a power base. Trotsky's superiority as a speaker and writer, and his greater intellectual gifts, counted for little when set against Stalin's grip on the Party machine. It is difficult to see how after 1924 Trotsky could have ever mounted a serious challenge to his rival. Even had his own particular failings not stopped him from acting at vital moments, Trotsky never had control of the political system as it operated in Soviet Russia. Politics is the art of the possible. After 1924 all the possibilities belonged to Stalin.

4 The Defeat of the Right

> **KEY ISSUE** What was the attitude of the Right on the issues of the NEP and industrialisation?

Although Stalin's victory over the Right Opposition is best studied as a feature of his industrialisation programme, it is important also to see it as the last stage in the consolidation of his authority over the Party and over the USSR. The defeat of the Right marks the end of any serious attempt to limit his power. From the late 1920s to his death in 1953 he would become increasingly dictatorial.

The major representatives of the Right were Rykov, the Chairman of the Central Committee, Tomsky, the leader of the trade unions, and Bukharin, the editor of *Pravda* and the outstanding economist in the Party. It had been these three who had loyally served Stalin in his outflanking of Trotsky and the Left. Politically the Right were by no means as challenging to Stalin as the Trotskyite bloc had been. What made Stalin move against them was that they stood in the way of the industrial and agricultural schemes that he began to implement in 1928.

Historians are uncertain as to when Stalin finally decided that the answer to the Soviet Union's growth problem was to impose collectivisation and industrialisation. It is unlikely to have been an early decision; the probability is that it was another piece of opportunism. Having defeated the Left politically he may then have felt free to adopt their economic policies. This would not have been mere perversity. Stalin had never fully committed himself on economic matters. His stance as a moderate had served its purpose in depicting his opponents as extremists. He was now in a position to judge policies on their economic merits, rather than as counters in the power game.

Some scholars have recently suggested that in 1928 Stalin became genuinely concerned about the serious grain shortage and decided that the only way to avoid a crisis was to resort to the drastic methods of collectivisation. It no longer mattered that this had been the very solution that the Left had advanced since they were now scattered.

For some time it had been the view of Bukharin and the Right that it was unnecessary to force the pace of industrialisation in the USSR. They argued that it would be less disruptive to let industry develop its own momentum. The State should assist, but it should not direct. Similarly, the peasants should not be controlled and oppressed; this would make them resentful and less productive. The Right agreed that it was from the land that the means of financing industrialisation would have to come, but they stressed that, by offering the peasants the chance to become prosperous, far more grain would be produced for sale abroad. Bukharin argued in the Politburo and at the Party Congress in 1928 that Stalin's aggressive policy of State grain procurements (enforced collections of fixed quotas) from the peasants was counter-productive. He declared that there were alternatives to these repressive policies. Bukharin was prepared to state openly what everybody knew, but was afraid to admit, that Stalin's programme was no different from the one that Trotsky had previously advocated.

The Right suffered from two fundamental weaknesses, one ideological, the other organisational. Their economic arguments were not unsound, but in the invasion-scare atmosphere of the late 1920s they appeared timid and unrealistic. The plea for a soft line with the peasants did not accord with the Party's needs. The threatening times were judged as requiring a dedicated resistance to the enemies of Revolution both within the USSR and outside. Stalin was able to suggest that the Right were guilty of underestimating the crisis facing the Party and the Soviet Union. He declared that it was a time for closing the ranks in keeping with the tradition of 1917. Here he showed a shrewd understanding of the mentality of Party members. The majority were far more likely to respond to the call for a return to a hard-line policy, such as had helped them survive the desperate days of the Civil War, than they were to risk the Revolution itself by untimely concessions to a peasantry that had no real place in the proletarian future. The Party of Marx and Lenin would not be well served by the policies of the Right.

The difficulty experienced by the Right in advancing their views was the same as that which had confronted the Left. How could they impress their ideas upon the Party while Stalin remained master of the Party's organisation? Bukharin and his colleagues wanted to remain good Party men and it was this sense of loyalty that weakened them in their attempts to oppose Stalin. Fearful of creating 'factionalism', they hoped that they could win the whole Party round to their way of thinking without causing deep divisions. On occasion they were sharply outspoken, Bukharin particularly so, but their basic approach was conciliatory. This played into Stalin's hands. Since it was largely his supporters who were responsible for drafting and distributing Party information, it was not difficult for Stalin to portray the Right as an irresponsible and dangerous clique.

The Right's only substantial support lay in the trade unions, whose Central Council was chaired by Tomsky, and in the CPSU's Moscow branch where Uglanov, an admirer of Bukharin, was the leader. When Stalin realised that these might be a source of opposition he acted quickly and decisively. He sent the ruthless and ambitious young Politburo member, Kaganovich, to undertake a purge of the suspect trade unionists; the Right proved totally incapable of organising resistance to this political *blitzkrieg*. Molotov, Stalin's faithful henchman, was dispatched to Moscow where he enlisted the support of the pro-Stalin members to effect a similar purge of the local Party officials.

By early 1929 Tomsky was no longer the national trade union leader, Uglanov had been replaced in the Moscow Party organisation, Rykov had been superseded as premier by Molotov, and Bukharin had been voted out as Chairman of the Comintern and had lost his place in the Politburo. Tomsky, Rykov and Bukharin, the main trio of the 'Right Opportunists' as they were termed by the Stalinist press, were allowed to remain in the Party but only after they had publicly admitted the error of their ways. Stalin's triumph over both Left and Right was complete. The grey blur was about to become the Red tsar.

References

1   J. V. Stalin, *Works* (Lawrence and Wishart, 1955), pp.115–16.
2   Leon Trotsky, *Stalin: An Appraisal of the Man and his Influence* (Hollis and Carter, 1947), pp.392–93.
3   in S. Hendel, *The Soviet Crucible* (Van Nostrand, 1959), p.281.
4   in Isaac Deutscher, *The Prophet Outcast: Trotsky 1929–40* (OUP, 1963), p.222.

Working on 'Stalin's Rise to Power'

A grasp of how Stalin came to power is basic to an understanding of the rest of this book. You need to be aware that there is an important connection between the power struggle just described, the economic issues covered in Chapter 3, and the foreign policy analysed in Chapter 5. The three areas to concentrate on in this chapter are the roots of Stalin's authority, his defeat of Trotsky and the Left, and his defeat of Bukharin and the Right. Be prepared throughout the book to use the Key Issues boxes. They are intended as more than a set of headings. Their aim is to alert you to the vital questions and to draw your attention to the issues with which historians grapple in this period. If you take them as your guide, you are unlikely to overlook any major themes.

Summary
Stalin: the Rise to Power, 1924–29

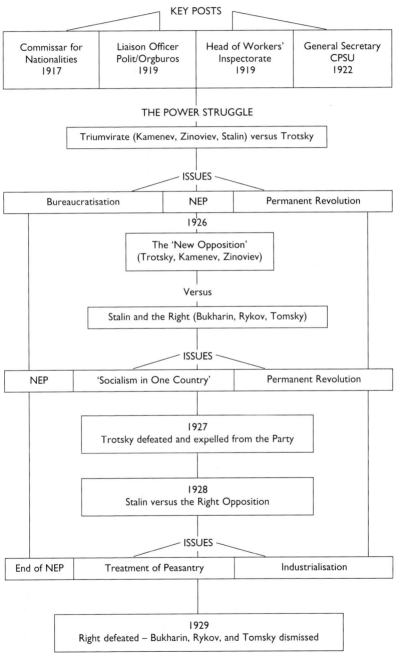

KEY POSTS

| Commissar for Nationalities 1917 | Liaison Officer Polit/Orgburos 1919 | Head of Workers' Inspectorate 1919 | General Secretary CPSU 1922 |

THE POWER STRUGGLE

Triumvirate (Kamenev, Zinoviev, Stalin) versus Trotsky

ISSUES

| Bureaucratisation | NEP | Permanent Revolution |

1926

The 'New Opposition'
(Trotsky, Kamenev, Zinoviev)

Versus

Stalin and the Right (Bukharin, Rykov, Tomsky)

ISSUES

| NEP | 'Socialism in One Country' | Permanent Revolution |

1927
Trotsky defeated and expelled from the Party

1928
Stalin versus the Right Opposition

ISSUES

| End of NEP | Treatment of Peasantry | Industrialisation |

1929
Right defeated – Bukharin, Rykov, and Tomsky dismissed

Answering structured and essay questions on Chapter 2

Structured questions are the type that begin with such leads as 'Describe ...', 'Describe how ...', 'Show how ...', 'In what ways did ...?' and 'Describe the ways in which ...' Typical questions based on the material in this chapter might be:

1. Describe the main features of Stalin's early life before 1917.
2. Show how the issue of the NEP divided the CPSU after the death of Lenin.
3. Describe the main steps taken by Stalin on his path to power between 1924 and 1929.
4. In what ways did Stalin's theory of 'socialism in one country' contrast with Trotsky's concept of 'permanent revolution'?
5. Describe the ways in which Stalin overcame the Left and Right opposition in the late 1920s.

The more difficult type of essay question either asks you to explain causation, that is to analyse why things occurred the way they did, or to make a judgment on a historical proposition. The questions on causation are usually in a 'why?' form with such leads as, 'Why was ...?', 'Explain why ...' and 'Account for ...'. Examples might be:

6. Why was Stalin in such a strong position in 1924 to begin his bid for power?
7. Account for Trotsky's failure to mount an effective challenge to Stalin in the 1920s.
8. Explain why the Right were no more successful than the new Left in their struggle with Stalin.

Examples of questions calling for your judgment might be:

9. How far do you agree that in the post-Lenin power struggle 'Trotsky was his own worst enemy'?
10. Examine the validity of the claim that Stalin's rise to power in the Soviet Union was 'a matter more of luck than judgement'.

Source-based questions on Chapter 2

To familiarise yourself with the type of question you are likely to be asked, study the following:

Lenin's legacy
Read the extracts from Lenin's Testament on page 16, from Stalin's speech on page 14, and from Trotsky's analysis on page 15,

1. **comprehension questions:** the type that test your basic understanding of the sources. Examples:

a) In his Testament, what reservations does Lenin have about Stalin, Trotsky, Zinoviev and Kamenev, and Bukharin individually? *(10 marks)*

b) In his speech at Lenin's funeral, what promises does Stalin make in regard to Party unity? *(6 marks)*

2. **stimulus questions:** the type that ask you to draw on your own knowledge to explain the meaning of a key concept or the role and/or importance of a key individual or institution. A typical question might be: What would you judge Stalin's purpose to have been in the funeral speech in constantly repeating Lenin's name? *(6 marks)*

3. **cross referencing questions:** the type that ask you to compare the content of two or more sources and reach a conclusion based on the comparison. A typical question might be: In what ways do these three sources differ or converge in the picture they present of Stalin's character? *(10 marks)*

4. **source evaluation questions:** the type that asks you to judge the usefulness and/or reliability of the sources. Typical questions might be:

a) How useful are these sources as evidence of the continuity between Lenin and Stalin? *(8 marks)*

b) How valuable are these sources to the historian who is studying the post-Lenin power struggle? *(10 marks)*

5. **lead-out questions:** the type that asks you to use one or two of the sources and your own knowledge to provide a historical explanation. A typical question might be: Using these sources, as well as your own knowledge, explain why Trotsky was eventually defeated in the power struggle. *(10 marks)*

3 Stalin and the Soviet Economy

POINTS TO CONSIDER

A grasp of economic developments is basic to an understanding of Russian history in the twentieth century. This applies with particular force to the Stalinist period. It was Stalin who created a 'second revolution' by wholly restructuring Soviet agriculture and industry, a move which had profound economic, social and political consequences. These are examined in the five main sections of the chapter. The first surveys the historical context of Stalin's changes. Section 2 describes the upheaval caused by the primary stage of Stalin's revolution – the enforced collectivisation of the peasantry. This is followed by a central section dealing with Stalin's essential industrial strategy, the five-year plans. The concluding sections, 4 and 5, deal with the performance of the Soviet economy in the war of 1941–45 and during Stalin's last years, 1945-53.

KEY DATES

1928	Collectivisation started.
	Beginning of the first FYP (Five Year Plan).
1932–33	Widespread famine in the USSR.
1933	Beginning of the second FYP.
1938	Beginning of the third FYP.
1941–45	The 'Great Patriotic War'.
1946	Beginning of the fourth FYP.
1951	Beginning of the fifth FYP.
1953	Death of Stalin.

1 Background

> **KEY ISSUE** In what sense was Stalin's economic strategy 'a revolution from above'?

Stalin's economic policy had one essential aim, the modernisation of the Soviet Union, and two essential methods, collectivisation and industrialisation. The collectivisation of agriculture, which substituted State ownership of the land for individual peasant-proprietorship, was a means to an end. It was intended to serve the needs of the industrialisation drive, which began with the introduction of the first Five-Year Plan (FYP) (1928–32). In 1929 Stalin defined collectivisation as 'the setting up of *kolkhozy* [collective farms] and *sovkhozy* [state farms] in order to squeeze out all capitalist elements from the land'. The *kolkhozy* were to be run as co-operatives in which the peasants would pool their resources and share the labour and the wages; the *sovkhozy* were to contain peasants working directly for the State, which would pay them a wage. In practice there were only minor differences between these two types of farm. Both were to be the means by which private peasant-ownership was ended and agriculture was made to serve the interests of the Soviet State. The plan was to group between 50 and 100 holdings into one unit. The reasoning was that large farms would be more efficient and would develop the effective use of agricultural machinery; the motorised tractor became the outstanding symbol of this proposed mechanising of Soviet farming. In addition to increasing the supply of cheap food for home consumption and sale abroad, efficient farming would decrease the number of rural workers needed and thus release them for the new factories.

The justification for Stalin's crash programme of collectivisation and industrialisation had been provided in 1926 by the critical resolution of the Party Congress of that year 'to transform our country from an agrarian into an industrial one, capable by its own efforts of producing the necessary means'. Stalin was to turn that resolution into reality. The Revolution in 1917 had succeeded in placing the Bolsheviks in power, but had not determined what their future policies should be; hence the arguments over the NEP, 'Permanent Revolution' and 'Socialism in One Country'. What Stalin's massive restructuring of agriculture and industry did was to put an end to uncertainty and argument. From 1928 onwards, with the introduction of collectivisation and industrialisation, there were no doubts concerning the Soviet Union's economic strategies and objectives. The Soviet State would take over the running of the nation's economy. This momentous decision is often referred to by historians as 'the second revolution'.

It is also frequently defined as a 'revolution from above'. To understand this description it is necessary to put Stalin's industrialisation drive in a Marxist context. In his analysis of the class war, Karl Marx had maintained that a society's political and social system was a direct product of its economic structure; it was on its economic base that its political and institutional super-structure rested. In theory, 1917 had been a revolution from below. The Bolshevik-led proletariat had begun the construction of a state in which the workers ruled. Bukharin and the Right had used this interpretation to argue that, since the USSR was now a proletarian society, the economy should be left to develop at its own pace, without interference from the government. But Stalin's economic programme from the late 1920s onwards totally inverted this process. He stood Marxist theory on its head. Instead of the economy determining the character of the political system, the political system would determine the character of the economy.

A central planning agency, known as *Gosplan*, had been introduced earlier under Lenin. However, what was different about Stalin's schemes was their scale, speed and intensity. Under Stalin, State control was to be total. Historians are still not entirely sure of Stalin's motivation. Before 1928 he had had no great reputation as an economic thinker and seems to have relied heavily on the theories of Evgeny Preobrazhensky, the leading economist among the Left Bolsheviks. The strongest probability is that Stalin saw in a hard-line policy the best means of confirming his authority over Party and government. When he introduced his radical economic changes Stalin claimed that they marked as significant a stage in Soviet Communism as had Lenin's fateful decision to begin the October rising in 1917. This comparison was obviously intended to enhance his own status as a revolutionary leader following in the footsteps of Lenin.

Yet it would be wrong to regard Stalin's policy as wholly a matter of political expediency. Judging from his speeches and actions after 1928, he had become convinced that the needs of Soviet Russia could be met only by the collectivisation and industrialisation programmes. That was the essence of his slogan 'Socialism in One Country'. The survival of the Revolution and of Soviet Russia depended on the nation's ability to turn itself into a modern industrial society within the shortest possible time. Stalin expressed this with particular clarity in 1931:

1 It is sometimes asked whether it is not possible to slow down the tempo somewhat, to put a check on the movement. No, comrades, it is not possible! The tempo must not be reduced! On the contrary we must increase it as much as is within our powers and possibilities. This
5 is dictated to us by our obligations to the working class of the whole world. To slacken the tempo would mean falling behind. And those who fall behind get beaten. But we do not want to be beaten.

No, we refuse to be beaten! One feature of old Russia was the continual beatings she suffered because of her backwardness. She was
10 beaten by the Mongol *khans*. She was beaten by the Turkish *beys*. She was beaten by the Polish and Lithuanian gentry. She was beaten by the British and French capitalists. She was beaten by the Japanese barons. All beat her – because of her backwardness, military backwardness, cultural backwardness, political backwardness, industrial backwardness,
15 agricultural backwardness. They beat her because to do so was profitable and could be done with impunity.

Do you remember the words of the pre-revolutionary poet: 'You are poor and abundant, mighty and powerless, Mother Russia'. Those gentlemen were quite familiar with the verses of the old poet. They
20 beat her, saying 'You are abundant, so one can enrich oneself at your expense'. They beat her, saying 'You are poor and powerless, so you can be beaten and plundered with impunity'. Such is the law of the exploiters – to beat the backward and weak. It is the jungle law of capitalism. You are backward, you are weak – therefore you are wrong;

25 hence you can be beaten and enslaved. You are mighty – therefore you
are right; hence we must be wary of you. That is why we must no
longer lag behind.
   We are fifty or a hundred years behind the advanced countries. We
30 must make good this distance in ten years. Either we do it, or we shall
be crushed. This is what our obligations to the workers and peasants of
the USSR dictate to us.[1]

This passionate appeal to Russian history subordinated everything to
the driving need for national survival. Stalin would later use this
appeal to justify the severity that accompanied the collectivisation of
Russian agriculture.

2 Collectivisation

> **KEY ISSUE** What purpose was the collectivisation of the peasantry
> intended to serve?

At its introduction in 1928, collectivisation was referred to as 'voluntary'.
Stalin claimed that it was the free choice of the peasants, but in practice
it was enforced on a very reluctant peasantry. Stalin had adopted the
ideas of the Left. He justified collectivisation by playing on the natural
antipathy of the Bolsheviks towards the peasants. In a major propaganda offensive, he identified a class of 'Kulaks', who were holding back
the workers' revolution. These Kulaks were defined as rich peasants who
had grown wealthy under the NEP. They monopolised the best land and
employed cheap peasant labour to farm it. By hoarding their farm produce they kept food prices high, thus making themselves rich at the
expense of the workers and poorer peasants. Unless they were broken
as a class, they would prevent the modernisation of the USSR.
   The concept of a Kulak class has been shown by scholars to have
been a Stalinist myth. The so-called Kulaks were really only those industrious peasants who, by their own efforts, had proved more efficient
farmers than their neighbours. In no sense did they constitute the class
of exploiting land-owners described in Stalin's propaganda campaign
against them. Nonetheless, given the tradition of landlord oppression
going back to tsarist times, the notion of a Kulak class proved a very
potent one and provided the grounds for the coercion of the peasantry
as a whole – middle and poor peasants, as well as Kulaks.
   Stalin defined his peasant policies in terms of Party principles.
Bolshevism was a proletarian creed. It taught that the days of the peasantry as a revolutionary social force had passed. The future belonged
to the urban workers. October 1917 had been the first stage in the
triumph of this proletarian class. Therefore, it was perfectly fitting
that the peasantry should, in a time of national crisis, become wholly

subservient to the demands of industrialisation. The USSR needed industrial investment and manpower. The land could provide both. Surplus grain would be sold abroad to raise investment funds for industry; surplus peasants would become factory workers.

One part of the formula was correct: for generations the Russian countryside had been overpopulated, creating a chronic land shortage. The other part was a gross distortion. There was no grain surplus. Indeed, even in the best years of the NEP, food production had seldom matched requirements. Yet Stalin insisted that the problem was not the lack of food but its inefficient distribution; food shortages were the result of grain-hoarding by the rich peasants. This argument was then used to explain the pressing need for collectivisation as a way of securing adequate food supplies. It also provided the moral grounds for the onslaught on the Kulaks, who were condemned as enemies of the Soviet nation in its struggle to modernise itself in the face of international, capitalist hostility.

In some regions 'de-Kulakisation' was undertaken with enthusiasm by the poorer peasants, since it provided them with an excuse to settle old scores and to give vent to local jealousies. Land and property were seized from the minority of better-off peasants, and they and their families were physically attacked. Such treatment was often the prelude to arrest and deportation by the official anti-Kulak squads, authorised by Stalin and modelled on the gangs which had persecuted the peasants during the State-organised Terror of the Civil War period (1918–20). The OGPU (the successor of the Cheka as the State security force) was entrusted with the recruitment and organisation of these squads.

The renewal of terror also served as a warning to the mass of the peasantry of the likely consequences of resisting the State reorganisation of Soviet agriculture. The destruction of the Kulaks was thus an integral part of the whole collectivisation process. As a Soviet official later admitted: 'most Party officers thought that the whole point of de-Kulakisation was its value as an administrative measure, speeding up tempos of collectivisation'.

In the period between December 1929 and March 1930, nearly 25% of the peasant farms in the USSR were collectivised. As a result, civil war broke out in the countryside. Peasants in their millions resisted. Such was the savagery and the degree of suffering that Stalin called a halt, blaming the troubles on over-zealous officials, 'dizzy with success'. Many of the peasants were allowed to return to their original holdings. However, the delay was only temporary. Having cleared his own name by blaming the difficulties on local officials, Stalin restarted collectivisation in a more determined, if somewhat slower, manner. The data on the next page indicates that by the end of the 1930s virtually the whole of the peasantry had been collectivised.

Behind these remarkable figures lay the story of a massive social upheaval. The peasants were disorientated and alienated. They either would not or could not co-operate in the deliberate destruction of their traditional way of life. The consequences were increasingly

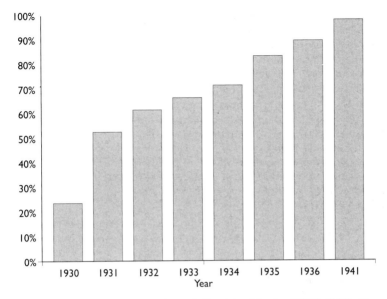

Percentage of Peasant Holdings Collectivised in the USSR, 1930–41

tragic. The majority of peasants ate their seed corn and slaughtered their livestock. There were no harvests left to reap or animals to rear. The Soviet authorities responded with still fiercer coercion, but this simply made matters worse: imprisonment, deportation and execution could not replenish the barns or restock the herds. The ignorance of farming techniques among those Party members (called the 'Twenty-five Thousand' after the number forming the first contingent) who were sent from the towns to restore food production levels, only added to the disruption. By a bitter irony, even as starvation set in, the little grain that was available was being exported as 'surplus' to obtain the foreign capital that industry demanded. By 1932 the situation on the land was catastrophic, as the following figures show.

The Fall in Food Consumption (in kilos per head)

	Bread	Potatoes	Meat & Lard	Butter
1928	250.4	141.1	24.8	1.35
1932	214.6	125.0	11.2	0.7

The Fall in Livestock

	Horses	Cattle	Pigs	Sheep and goats
1928	33 million	70 million	26 million	146 million
1932	15 million	34 million	9 million	42 million

These figures refer to the USSR as a whole. In the urban areas there was relatively more food available. Indeed, a major purpose of the grain requisition squads was to maintain adequate supplies to the industrial regions. This meant that the misery in the countryside was proportionally greater, with areas such as the Ukraine and Kazhakstan suffering particularly severely. The devastation experienced by the Kazhaks can be gauged from the statistic that in this period they lost nearly 90 per cent of their livestock.

Starvation, which in many parts of the Soviet Union persisted throughout the 1930s, was at its worst in the years 1932–33, when there occurred a national famine. Collectivisation led to despair among large sections of the peasantry. In many areas of the USSR the uprooted peasants simply stopped producing, either as an act of desperate resistance or through sheer inability to adapt to the bewilderingly new and violently enforced regime. Few peasants understood the economic thinking, still less the ideological justification, behind it. The harsh fact was that, as a subordinate part of a grand industrial design, Soviet agriculture had been burdened with a task that it could not fulfil. The result was that for a significant period it ceased in any meaningful sense to function at all. So great was the migration from the rural to the urban areas that a system of internal passports was introduced in an effort to control the flow. Some idea of the horrors can be obtained from the following contemporary accounts:

I Trainloads of deported peasants left for the icy North, the forests, the steppes, the deserts. These were whole populations, denuded of everything; the old folk starved to death in mid-journey, new-born babes were buried on the banks of the roadside, and each wilderness had its
5 little cross of boughs or white wood. Other populations dragging all their mean possessions on wagons, rushed towards the frontiers of Poland, Rumania, and China and crossed them – by no means intact, to be sure – in spite of the machine guns … Agricultural technicians and experts were brave in denouncing the blunders and excesses; they
10 were arrested in thousands and made to appear in huge sabotage trials so that responsibility might be unloaded on somebody.[2]

I Along with the peasants who flock to the towns because there is no hope of survival in the country, there are children who are simply brought here and abandoned by their parents who then return to their village to die … A medical team [in the Kharkiv region] does a sort of
5 selection process. Anyone who is not yet swollen up and still has a chance of survival is directed to the Kholodnoya Gora buildings, where a constant population of about 8,000 lies dying on straw beds in the big hangars. Most of them are children. People who are already starting to swell up are moved out in goods trains and abandoned forty miles out
10 of town so that they can die out of sight. When they arrive at the destination, huge ditches are dug, and the dead are carried out of the wagons.[3]

Despite such evidence of the tragedy that had overtaken the USSR, the official Stalinist line was that there was no famine. In the whole of the contemporary Soviet press there were only two oblique references to it. This conspiracy of silence was of more than political significance. As well as protecting the image of Stalin the great planner, it effectively prevented the introduction of measures to remedy the distress. Since the famine did not officially exist, Soviet Russia could not publicly take steps to relieve it. For the same reason it could not appeal, as had been done during an earlier Russian famine in 1921, for aid from the outside world. Thus, what Isaac Deutscher, the historian and former Trotskyist, called 'the first purely man-made famine in history' went unacknowledged in order to avoid discredit falling on Stalin. Not for the last time, a large proportion of the Soviet people was sacrificed on the altar of Stalin's reputation. There was a strong rumour that Stalin's second wife, Nadezdha Alliluyeva, had been driven to suicide by the knowledge that it was her husband's brutal policies that had caused the famine. Shortly before her death she had railed at Stalin: 'You are a tormentor, that's what you are. You torment your own son. You torment your wife. You torment the whole Russian people.'⁴

De-Stalinisation in the 1950s revealed Stalin's crimes against the Party (see page 112). However, it was not until the 1980s that Stalin's offences against the Russian people began to be publicly admitted in the USSR. In 1989 the Soviet historian, Dmitri Volkogonov produced the first unexpurgated Russian biography of Joseph Stalin. Volkogonov confirmed many of the suspicions long entertained in the West of his inhumanity. Of special interest in relation to the collectivisation period was Volkogonov's discovery from official Soviet records that Stalin went into the countryside on only one occasion, in 1928, and visited a factory only twice.

It is difficult to justify collectivisation even on economic grounds. Historians find little evidence that it provided the Soviet Union with the growth in capital that had been one of the pretexts for its introduction. The truth was that there was never a genuine food surplus that could be sold to raise capital. Although the famine had eased by 1939, agriculture continued to produce less than was required to feed the Soviet population. Despite an increase in grain production, stocks of other food stuffs declined. There is broad agreement among modern economic analysts that a policy of state taxation of an uncollectivised peasantry would have produced a much higher level of investment capital, while avoiding the social dislocation and misery of Stalin's measures. (This was the very policy that had been urged by Bukharin and the Right.)

It has also been suggested that if, instead of trying to increase grain production by fighting a class war, Stalin and his officials had encouraged the peasants to adopt common-sense methods, such as using rat poison and ventilating their barns adequately, the consequent saving

An anti-Kulak demonstration on a collective farm in 1930. The banner reads: 'Liquidate the Kulaks as a class'.

of food stocks would have made collectivisation unnecessary. This, of course, overlooks the ideological dimension of Stalin's land programme and gives no place to his deep sense of vindictiveness towards the Russian peasantry.

Even allowing for the occasional progressive aspect of collectivisation, such as the spread of the Machine Tractor Stations (MTS), the overall picture remains bleak. By 1939 Soviet agricultural productivity had barely returned to the level recorded for tsarist Russia in 1913. But the most damning consideration still remains the man-made famine, which in the 1930s killed between ten and fifteen million peasants.

3 Industrialisation

> **KEY ISSUE** How close did the Five-Year Plans come to achieving Stalin's aims for Soviet industry?

Stalin's programme of industrialisation for the USSR is best understood as an attempt to establish a war economy. He declared that he was promoting a great leap forward, as a war on the failings of Russia's past, as a war against the class enemies within, and as a preparation for war against the nation's capitalist enemies abroad. His martial imagery helps to explain the form that Soviet industrialisation took. For Stalin, industry meant heavy industry. He saw the production of iron, steel, and oil as the genuine measure of industrial growth, as it was these that provided the sinews of war. He believed that the industrial revolutions in Europe and North America had been based on iron and steel production. So, the USSR must adopt a similar industrial pattern in its drive towards modernisation. The difference would be that, whereas the West had taken the capitalist road, the USSR would follow the path of socialism.

This was not mere rhetoric. It has to be remembered that Stalin's industrialisation drive in the 1930s coincided with the Depression in the Western world, a period of economic stagnation which was interpreted by Marxists as marking the final collapse of capitalism. Stalin claimed that the USSR was introducing into her own economy the proven technical successes of Western industrialisation but was rejecting the self-destructive capitalist system that went with them. By socialist-inspired choice the USSR would avoid the errors that had begun to undermine the Western economies. This gave plausibility to Stalin's concept of a planned economy for the Soviet Union.

The character of industrialisation under Stalin is best studied in relation to the Five-Year Plans (FYPs). These were a series of programmes for industrial expansion, expressed as production targets. *Gosplan*, the State planning-authority, was required by Stalin to draw up a list of quotas ranging across the whole of Soviet industry. The process began in 1928 and, allowing for the intervention of the war years 1941–45, lasted until Stalin's death in 1953. There were five separate Plans:

1st FYP	October, 1928 to December, 1932
2nd FYP	January, 1933 to December, 1937
3rd FYP	January, 1938 to June, 1941
4th FYP	January, 1946 to December, 1950
5th FYP	January, 1951 to December, 1955

a) The First Five-Year Plan, 1928–32

The term 'Plan' is misleading. A set of objectives is by no means the same thing as a plan. Indeed real planning was the key element missing from the first FYP. It provided detailed production figures but said little about how they were to be achieved. It simply assumed the quotas would be met. What the first FYP represented, therefore, was a set of ideal targets, which bore little relation to reality. As with collectivisation, so with industrialisation: local officials and managers laundered their production figures in order to give the impression of greater success than had actually been achieved. For this reason precise statistics for the first FYP are difficult to determine. A further complication is that three quite distinct versions of the first FYP eventually appeared. Impressed by the apparent progress of the Plan in its early stages, Stalin encouraged the formulation of an 'optimal' plan which reassessed targets upwards. These new quotas were hopelessly unrealistic and stood no chance of being reached. Nonetheless, on the basis of the supposed achievements of this 'optimal' plan the figures were revised still higher. As shown on page 41, Western analysts have calculated alternative or 'actual' figures.

The importance of these figures should not be exaggerated. At the time it was the overall design, not the detail, that mattered. Essentially the Plan was a huge propaganda project which aimed at convincing the Soviet people that they were engaged in a vast industrial enterprise of their own making. By their own efforts, they were changing the shape and character of the society in which they lived, making it safe from foreign invasion and providing it with the means of achieving greatness. Nor were they all forced into line. The coercion that was widely used has tended to blind foreign observers to the idealism that inspired many of the participants in Soviet Russia's headlong drive for industrialisation. There was, among the young especially, an enthusiasm and a commitment that suggested that many Soviet citizens believed they were genuinely building a new and better society.

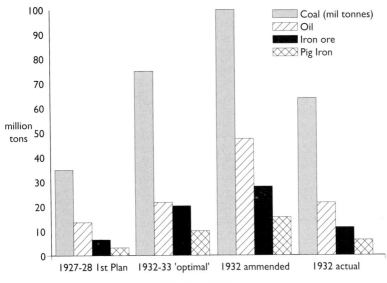

The First FYP

The term 'cultural revolution' is an appropriate description of the scale and significance of what was being undertaken under Stalin's leadership. Two renowned Western analysts of Soviet affairs, Alec Nove and Sheila Fitzpatrick, have laid stress on this aspect. They see behind the economic changes of this period a real attempt being made to create a new type of individual, what was called at the time *Homo Sovieticus* (Soviet man), as if a new species had come into being. Stalin told a gathering of Soviet writers that they should regard themselves as 'engineers, directing the reconstruction of the human soul'.

The sense of the Soviet people as masters of their own fate was expressed in the slogan, 'There is no fortress that we Bolsheviks cannot storm'. John Scott, an American Communist and one of the many pro-Soviet Western industrial advisers who came to the USSR at this time, was impressed by the mixture of idealism and coercion that characterised the early stages of Stalinist industrialisation. He described how the city of Magnitogorsk was built from scratch:

1 Within several years, half a billion cubic feet of excavation was done, forty-two million cubic feet of reinforced concrete poured, five million cubic feet of fire bricks laid, a quarter of a million tons of structured steel erected. This was done without sufficient labour, without necess-
5 ary quantities of the most elementary materials. Brigades of young enthusiasts from every corner of the Soviet Union arrived in the summer of 1930 and did the groundwork of railroad and dam construction necessary. Later, groups of local peasants and herdsmen came to Magnitogorsk because of bad conditions in the villages, due to col-

10 lectivisation. Many of the peasants were completely unfamiliar with industrial tools and processes ... A colony of several hundred foreign engineers and specialists, some of whom made as high as one hundred dollars a day, arrived to advise and direct the work ...

From 1928 until 1932 nearly a quarter of a million people came to
15 Magnitogorsk. About three quarters of these new arrivals came of their own free will seeking work, bread-cards, better conditions. The rest came under compulsion.[5]

It was by such efforts that the first FYP gained its results. After due account has been taken of the falsification of returns, the Plan still remains an extraordinary, if patchy, achievement. Coal, iron, and the generation of electrical power all increased in huge proportions. The production of steel and chemicals (particularly in the key area of fertilisers) was less impressive, while the output of finished textiles actually declined. Not surprisingly, in view of the disruption caused by collectivisation, village-based handicrafts largely died out. By deliberate design, the production of consumer articles was given a low priority. The harshness of the Soviet authorities was also evident in their reluctance to pay more than passing attention to living conditions in the overcrowded industrial centres. The supply of accommodation, sub-standard even by the traditionally poor quality of Russian urban housing, failed to meet demand. This neglect of basic social needs was not accidental. The Plan had never been intended to raise living standards. Its purpose was collective, not individual. It called for sacrifice and dedication on the part of the workers in the construction of a socialist state, able to sustain itself economically and militarily against the enmity of the capitalist world.

Stalin's presentation of the FYP as a defence of the USSR against international hostility enabled him to brand resistance to the Plan as 'sabotage'. A series of public trials of industrial 'wreckers', including a number of foreign workers, was used to impress the Party and the masses of the futility of protesting against the industrialisation programme. In 1928 in a prelude to the first FYP, Stalin claimed to have discovered an anti-Soviet conspiracy among the mining engineers of Shakhty in the Donbass region. Their subsequent public trial was intended to cow the industrial workforce. It also showed that the privileged position of the skilled workers, the 'bourgeois experts', was to be tolerated no longer.

This attack upon the existing managerial elite was part of a pattern in the first FYP which emphasised quantity at the expense of quality. The push was towards sheer volume of industrial output, almost as a self-justifying activity that would prove the correctness of Stalin's grand economic schemes. Sheila Fitzpatrick has termed this 'gigantomania', the worship of size for its own sake. The quality of the output was not regarded as the measure of success. This may be interpreted as a shrewd judgement on Stalin's part. He knew that the untrained peasants who poured into such places as Magnitogorsk would not

'The Five-Year Plan' – a propaganda wall poster of the 1930s, depicting Stalin as the heroic creator of a powerful, industrialised, Soviet Union. He is overcoming the forces of religion, international capitalism, and Russian conservatism and backwardness.

turn immediately into skilled workers. It made sense, therefore, at least in the short term, to shelve the question of efficiency and quality control and to emphasise the economic values of prodigious collective endeavour. Stories circulated regarding machines, factories, and even whole enterprises being ruined because of the workers' ignorance of elementary industrial procedures. These descriptions illustrated the problems that arose from basing an industrial revolution on a workforce that was essentially rural and conservative.

Stalin's notions of industrial 'saboteurs' and 'wreckers' allowed him to place the blame for inefficiency and under-production on managers and workers who were not prepared to play their proper part in the transformation of Soviet society. OGPU agents and Party *cadres* (political officers) were sent into the factories and onto the construction sites to spy on managers and workers and to report back on their performance.

Once again, political control became the instrument for enforcing economic policy. 'Sabotage' became a blanket term used to denounce anyone considered to be less than wholly committed to the new Soviet order. The simplest errors, such as being late for work, damaging tools, or miscounting items, became a pretext for condemning the unfortunate perpetrator for being opposed to socialist progress. At a higher level, those factory managers or foremen who proved incapable of fulfilling their production quotas might find themselves on public trial as enemies of the Soviet state. In such an atmosphere, fear and recrimination flourished. Doctoring official returns and inflating output figures became normal practice. Everybody at every level was engaged in a huge game of fraud. This was why the Soviet statistics for industrial growth were so unreliable and why it was possible for Stalin to claim in midcourse that since the first FYP had already met its initial targets, it would be shortened to a four year plan. In Stalin's industrial revolution appearances were everything. This was where the logic of 'gigantomania' had led.

The industrial policies of this time were described as 'the Stalinist blue-print' or 'Stalin's economic model'. Modern scholars are, however, wary of using such terms. Norman Stone, for example, interprets Stalin's policies not as far-sighted strategy but as 'simply putting one foot in front of the other as he went along'. In no real sense was the first FYP a blue-print or model, if by that is meant a detailed programme of industrial expansion. Despite the growing tendency in all official Soviet documents of the 1930s to include a fulsome reference to Stalin, the master-planner, there was in fact very little planning from the top. Broad objectives were declared and heavy emphasis was placed upon certain types of industrial product, but the methods of achieving these targets were left to be worked out by officials and managers on the spot. Stalin's government exhorted, cajoled, and terrorised the workforce into ever greater efforts towards ever greater production, but such planning as there was occurred not at nation but at local level. It was the regional and site managers who, struggling desperately to make sense of the instructions they were given from on high, formulated the actual schemes to meet their given production quotas. This was why it was so easy for Stalin and his Kremlin colleagues to accuse lesser officials of sabotage while themselves avoiding any taint of incompetence.

b) The Second and Third Five-Year Plans (1933–37, 1938–41)

The Second FYP, which was begun during the grimmest period of the agricultural famine, was more realistic than the First. Nevertheless, it still revealed the unco-ordinated nature of much of the central planning. Over-production occurred in some parts of the economy, underproduction in others, with the frequent result that whole branches of industry were held up for lack of essential supplies. The struggle to obtain an adequate supply of materials often led to fierce competition between regions and sectors of industry, all of them anxious to escape the charge of failing to achieve the goals laid down from above. In consequence, there was much unproductive hoarding of resources and a lack of the co-operation necessary for integrated industrial growth. Complaints about poor standards, thinly veiled in order to avoid appearing critical of Stalin and the Plan, continued to be made.

The reluctance to expose weaknesses in the Plan hindered genuine industrial growth. Since no one was willing to admit that an error in planning or production had taken place, faults went unchecked until they reached proportions that could no longer be hidden. There followed the inevitable search for scapegoats. It was in the period of the Second and Third FYPs that Stalin's political purges were at their fiercest; in such an all-pervading atmosphere of terror the mere accusation of 'sabotage' was taken as a proof of guilt. Productivity suffered in consequence. As Alec Nove observes: 'Everywhere there were said to be spies, wreckers, diversionists. There was a grave shortage of qualified personnel, so the deportation of many thousands of engineers and technologists to distant concentration camps represented a severe loss'.[6]

What successes there were occurred again in heavy industry where the Second FYP began to reap the benefit of the creation of large-scale plants under the First Plan. Despite Stalin's statements to the contrary, the living standards of the workers failed to rise. This was due, in part, to the effects of the famine, but also to the continuing neglect in the Plans of consumer goods. Beyond the comfort to be gained from feeling that they were engaged in a great national enterprise, a theme constantly emphasised in the Soviet press, there were few material rewards to help the workers endure the severity of their conditions. Moreover, they had to accept their lot without complaint. The official line was that all was well.

The Party's control of newspapers, cinema and radio meant that only a favourable view of the Plans and their achievements was ever presented. A remarkable example of this was the Stakhanovite movement that began in 1935. It was officially claimed in August of that year that Alexei Stakhanov, a miner in the Donbass region, had produced in one five-hour shift over fourteen times his required quota of coal. Whatever the truth of the story, his feat was seized on by the authorities as a glorious example of what was possible in a Soviet Union guided by the great and wise Joseph Stalin. Soviet workers were now to be inspired or shamed into raising their production norms yet higher. Ironically, while many workers did respond positively to the 'Stakhanovite' call for greater output, the fact that they could do so was a sign of how low existing productivity levels had been.

It is a striking paradox that in a professedly proletarian state the living standards of the Soviet workers should have been given the lowest place in the order of planning priorities. The explanation has two main aspects: the weakness of the trade unions and the character of the Soviet 'war economy'. After 1917, the Russian trade unions had declined into powerlessness. According to Bolshevik theory, in a truly socialist state such as Russia now was, there was no distinction between the interests of government and those of the workers. Therefore, there was no longer any need for a separate trade union movement. In 1920 Trotsky had taken formal steps to destroy the independence of the unions and bring them directly under Bolshevik control. The result was that after 1920 the unions were simply the means by which the Bolshevik government enforced its requirements upon the workers.

Under Stalin's industrialisation programme any semblance of workers' rights disappeared. Strikes were not permitted and the traditional demands for better pay and conditions were regarded as selfishly inappropriate in a time of national crisis. A code of 'labour discipline' was drawn up, demanding maximum effort and output; failure to conform could be punished by a range of penalties from loss of wages to imprisonment in forced labour camps. On paper, wages improved during the Second FYP, but in real terms, given the continuance of food rationing and high prices, living standards were lower in 1937 than they had been in 1928.

The official line was that the sacrifice this entailed was justified by the crisis facing the USSR. Throughout the period of the FYPs, the Soviet government asserted that the nation was under siege. It claimed that unless priority was given to defence needs, the continued existence of the USSR could not be guaranteed. Set against such a threat, workers' material interests were of little significance. To demand improved living and working conditions at a time when the Soviet Union was fighting for survival was characterised as national betrayal. Food shortages continued, severe overcrowding persisted and basic consumer goods remained unavailable; but expenditure on armaments increased. Between 1933 and 1937, defence spending rose from 4 to 17 per cent of the overall industrial budget. By 1940, under the terms of the Third FYP, which renewed the commitment to heavy industrial development, this proportion had reached 33 per cent.

Despite the official adulation of Stalin for his great diplomatic triumph in achieving the non-aggression Pact with Nazi Germany in August 1939 (see page 88), there was no relaxation within the Soviet Union of the war atmosphere. Indeed, the conditions of the ordinary people became even harsher. An official decree of 1940 abolished what remained of the free labour market. Government direction of labour, restrictions on population movement, enforced settlement of undeveloped areas, and severe penalties for slacking and absenteeism were some of the measures imposed under this regulation. In 1941, when the German invasion effectively destroyed the Third FYP, the conditions of the Soviet industrial workers were marginally lower than in 1928. Yet whatever the privations of the workers, the fact was that in 1941 the USSR was in a position economically to engage in a successful military struggle of unprecedented intensity. In Soviet propaganda, this was what mattered, not minor questions of living standards. The USSR's triumph over Nazism would later be claimed as the ultimate proof of the wisdom of Stalin's enforced industrialisation programme.

In judging the scale of Stalin's achievement it is helpful to cite such statistics relating to industrial output during the period of the first three FYPs as are reliable. The following data are drawn from the work of the economic historian E. Zaleski, whose findings are based on careful analysis of Soviet and Western sources:

	1927	1930	1932	1935	1937	1940
Coal (million tons)	35	60	64	100	128	150
Steel (million tons)	3	5	6	13	18	18
Oil (million tons)	12	17	21	24	26	26
Electricity (million Kilowatt hours)	18	22	20	45	80	90

4 The Economy in Wartime, 1941–45

> **KEY ISSUE** How effectively did the Soviet economy respond to the demands of war?

The ferocious four-year war that began with the German invasion of the USSR in June 1941 destroyed any possibility of measured planning.

Henceforward all considerations, whether political or economic, were subordinated to the sheer necessity of survival. After an initial paralysis of will, Stalin again began to exercise his formidable powers of leadership. In his first radio broadcast of the war (3 July 1941) he exhorted the people to defend 'Mother Russia' by adopting the scorched-earth methods of warfare that had always saved the nation in its glorious past:

1   The issue is one of life and death for the soviet State, of life and death for the peoples of the USSR. We must mobilise ourselves and reorganise all our work on a new wartime footing, where there can be no mercy to the enemy.

5   We must strengthen the Red Army's rear, subordinating all our work to this end. All our industries must be made to work with greater intensity, to produce more rifles, machine-guns, cartridges, shells, planes; we must organise the guarding of factories, power stations, telephonic and telegraphic communications, and arrange local air-raid protection.

10   In case of a forced retreat of Red Army units, all rolling stock must be evacuated; the enemy must not be left a single engine, a single railway car, not a single pound of grain or gallon of fuel. The collective farmers must drive off all their cattle and turn over their grain to the safe keeping of the state authorities for transportation to the rear. All

15   valuable property, including non-ferrous metals, grain and fuel, that cannot be withdrawn must be destroyed without fail.

In areas occupied by the enemy, sabotage groups must be organised to combat enemy units, to foment guerrilla warfare everywhere, to blow up bridges and roads, damage telephone and telegraph lines, to set

20   fire to forests, stores and transports. In occupied regions, conditions must be made unbearable for the enemy.[7]

After 1941, Stalin's previous insistence that the Soviet economy be put on a war footing began to show obvious benefits. Whatever the reality of central planning had been, the principle of centralised authority was of considerable value when it came to organising the war effort. Furthermore, the harshness of the conditions under which the Soviet people had laboured in the 1930s had prepared them for the fearful hardships of war. In the four bitter years of 'The Great Patriotic War' of 1941 to 1945, the raw courage and resilience of the Russian people, seemingly inured to suffering, proved a priceless asset. The outstanding example of this was the Soviet victory in 1943 at Stalingrad, which proved the turning point in the war on the eastern front. In the battle which occupied the winter months of 1942–43 over a million Soviet troops were killed. The life expectancy of a soldier at the front was twenty-four hours.

How much the Soviet people suffered can be expressed very simply. At the end of 1941, after only six months of war, nearly half the Soviet population and over a third of the national's industrial plant was under German occupation; 60 per cent of iron and steel production, 40 per cent of the railway system, 60 per cent of livestock, and 40 per cent of grain stocks had been lost. The reason for this early catastrophe was that under the FYPs Soviet industrial expansion had been sited west of the Urals, the area most vulnerable to German attack. Extraordinary, and largely successful, efforts were then made to transfer whole sectors of Soviet industry to the relative safety of the eastern USSR. Military conscription of all adult males not involved in essential war work, and war casualties (four million in the first year of the war), meant that women and children had to fill the vacant places in the factories. Work on the land became an almost totally female activity. Arms production received top priority. By 1942 over half of the national income was being devoted to military expenditure. This was the highest proportion by far of any of the countries involved in the Second World War. In such straitened circumstances the pre-war levels of production could not be maintained. The following figures suggest the degree of industrial disruption in the Soviet Union caused by the German occupation during the first two years of the war:

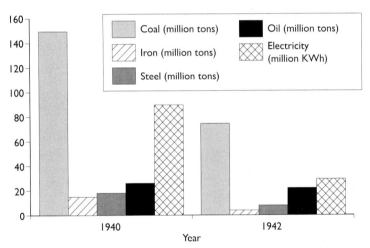

Industrial Production in the USSR

1942 marked the lowest point in Soviet economic fortunes. But from then on, as things began to improve on the military front, there was a corresponding improvement in the economy. The new factories in the Urals began to come into production. The supplies sent by the USA to the USSR under a lend-lease programme bolstered the Soviet's home-produced supply of weapons and motor transport. Of special significance was the recovery and expansion of the Soviet railway system, which enabled troops and supplies to be moved strategically. With the retreat of the German armies on a broad front, following major Soviet victories in 1943 at Stalingrad and Kursk, the USSR began to regain its lost industrial sites. The scale of economic recovery that followed can be seen in the accompanying table.

Wartime Productivity in the USSR
(calculated to a base unit of 100 in 1940)

	1941	1942	1943	1944
National Income	92	66	74	88
Total Industrial Output	98	77	90	104
Armaments Production	140	186	224	251
Fuel Production	94	53	59	75
Agricultural Output	42	38	37	54

These figures indicate the prodigious response of the Soviet Union to the demands of war. The ability to achieve a huge arms production at a time of acute shortages in plant, materials and manpower is the outstanding example of this response. However, the recovery was achieved at the expense of even greater privation for the Soviet people than they had already borne during collectivisation and industrialisation. The long German occupation of the most fertile land, the shortage of agricultural labour, the re-imposition of State grain and livestock requisitions, and the breakdown of the food distribution system – all these combined to transform the chronic Russian food shortage into famine. Over a quarter of the estimated 25 million fatalities suffered by the Soviet Union during the war were the result of starvation. Even so, Stalin had the last word. As the military struggle drew to its successful close in May 1945, he declared: 'We have survived the most cruel and hardest of all wars ever experienced in the history of our Motherland. The point is that the Soviet social system has proved to be more capable of life and more stable than a non-Soviet system.'

5 Post-War Reconstruction

KEY ISSUE What were Stalin's post-war economic aims?

Triumph in war did not lessen the suffering of the Soviet people or make them freer. Stalin's grip upon the country became still tighter. The Soviet victory and his part in it made his position within the USSR unassailable. When Stalin turned to the question of Soviet economic reconstruction after the ravages of war, it was with no thought of rewarding the people for their efforts. If anything, he was even more suspicious of the outside world than he had been before 1941. He called upon the nation to redouble its efforts. Defence and the expansion of heavy industry were again to be the priorities. Little appeared to have changed in his economic thinking since 1928. Minor adjustments were made in the structure of the central planning departments, but the basic economic strategy remained the same.

At the end of the war the Soviet Union was in a potentially strong economic position. The recovery of all its previously occupied territory, its entitlement to large-scale reparations from defeated Germany, and its hold over the Eastern European states it claimed to have liberated during the war, had considerably increased its material resources. However, against that had to be set the degree of disruption caused by the war. The Fourth FYP (1946–50) was aimed at restoring production to the levels of 1941. Even allowing for inflated claims, this seems to have been largely achieved within three years. But, as had been the case with the earlier Plans, the goals were reached only in the traditional areas of heavy industry. The Soviet economy itself remained unbalanced. In those sectors where unskilled and forced labour could be easily used, as in war-damage clearance and the re-building of abandoned factories and plants, the results were impressive.

However, there was little recognition of the need to adapt to progressive industrial techniques, despite the presence in the USSR after the war of United Nations economic advisers who were sympathetic to Soviet needs. Stalin continued to favour large-scale construction projects. Bridges, dams, refineries, and generating plants took pride of place in the Plan, but with little thought being given to their integration into an overall economic strategy. Their construction often involved the wasting of vital financial and material resources that could have been invested far more productively elsewhere. These showpieces, collectively termed 'Stalin's Grand Projects of Communism', had more to do with propaganda than economic planning. The same consideration may be said to apply to the successful detonation in 1949 of the Soviet Union's first atomic weapon.

When such reservations have been made, it remains the case that by 1950 the Fourth FYP had realised its objectives in regard to the growth of heavy industry; the output of iron and steel, oil and electrical power had been doubled. The major weakness, as with the pre-war Plans, was the inability to increase agricultural productivity or to raise the living standards of the Soviet workers. Lip service was paid to these two aims in both the Fourth and Fifth FYPs (the latter, 1951–55, outliving Stalin), but, in practice, hardly anything was done. Agriculture continued to be under-capitalised and regarded as wholly secondary to the needs of industry. When Khrushchev was given a special commission in the early 1950s to investigate problems on the collective farms, he spent more time in enforcing political control in the countryside than in improving food yields. Rationing had been formally ended in 1947 but this was not a real sign that shortages had been overcome; a widespread black-market, officially condemned but tolerated in practice, was necessary for the workers to supplement their meagre resources. Accommodation was scarcer and conditions in the factories were grimmer than they had been in wartime. Real wages were not permitted to rise above subsistence level and the rigours of the 'Labour Code' were not relaxed. When Stalin died in 1953 the lot of the Russian worker, the concept of whose material improvement had been the inspiration of the October Revolution, was harsher than at any time since 1917.

References

1   J. V. Stalin, *Works* (Lawrence and Wishart, 1955), vol 13, pp.40–41.
2   Victor Serge, *Memoirs of a Revolutionary 1901–1941* (OUP, 1963), pp.246–48.
3   From a description by the Italian consul in Kharkiv, in Andrea Graziosi, *The Great Soviet Peasant War: Bolsheviks and Peasants, 1917–33* (Harvard University Press, 1996), pp.59-60.
4   A. Orlov, *The Secret History of Stalin's Crimes* (1954), quoted in Piers Brendon, *The Dark Valley: A Panorama of the 1930s* (Jonathan Cape, 2000), p.213.
5   John Scott, *Behind the Urals* (Secker and Warburg, 1942), p.52–54.
6   Alec Nove, *An Economic History of the USSR* (Penguin, 1972).
7   *Stalin, War Speeches, Orders of the Day, and Answers to Foreign Press Correspondents during the Great Patriotic War* (Hutchinson, 1946), p.6.

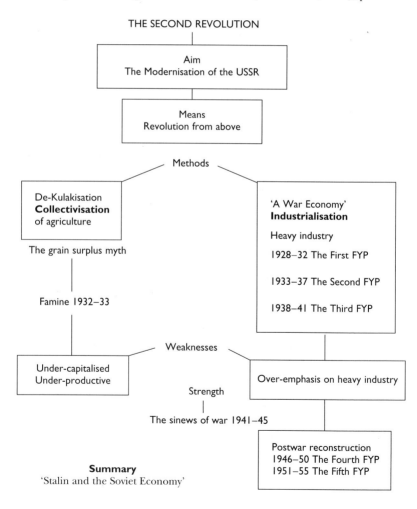

THE SECOND REVOLUTION

Aim
The Modernisation of the USSR

Means
Revolution from above

Methods

De-Kulakisation
Collectivisation
of agriculture

The grain surplus myth

Famine 1932–33

'A War Economy'
Industrialisation

Heavy industry

1928–32 The First FYP

1933–37 The Second FYP

1938–41 The Third FYP

Weaknesses

Under-capitalised
Under-productive

Over-emphasis on heavy industry

Strength

The sinews of war 1941–45

Postwar reconstruction
1946–50 The Fourth FYP
1951–55 The Fifth FYP

Summary
'Stalin and the Soviet Economy'

Working on Chapter 3

The economic changes associated with Stalin's policies after 1928 mark a significant turning-point in the development of modern Russia. The introduction of collectivisation and industrialisation created 'the Second Revolution', a term which suggests that these processes were as important as the Revolution of 1917 itself. Your aim, therefore, is to show an awareness of the major economic questions facing Stalin's Russia. How was a revolutionary country which had rejected capitalism to survive in a capitalist world? How could the Soviet Union best use its resources to ensure that survival? Could a country that was predominantly rural and agricultural be transformed into a modern industrial state? Such questions lay at the heart of Soviet politics. Stalin's personal role is, of course, vital and it makes sense for you to concentrate on the central theme: what were Stalin's economic aims and how far did he achieve them? In pursuing these questions you will necessarily have to study all the essential features of the Russian economy between 1928 and 1953.

Answering structured and essay questions on Chapter 3

Structured questions:
1. Describe the main ways in which the collectivisation of the Russian peasantry was introduced.
2. In what ways was Soviet industry reorganised under the First FYP?
3. Show how the Soviet economy was reshaped to meet the demands of the 1941–45 war.

Examples of essay questions on causation:
4. Why were the Kulaks made a particular target during the enforcement of collectivisation?
5. Why did the First FYP lay such stress on heavy industry?
6. Explain why the living standards of the Soviet workers declined during the period of the FYPs.

Examples of essay questions calling for your judgement:
7. In what sense did the policies of collectivisation and industrialisation constitute 'a Second Revolution' in the Soviet Union?
8. How accurate is it to describe the First Five-Year Plan (1928–32) as an 'economic model'?
9. How valid is the view that the USSR survived the war of 1941–45 because Stalin had successfully reconstructed the Soviet economy by 1941?

Source-Based Questions on Chapter 3

Study Stalin's speech of 1931 on page 32, the table of figures on the First FYP on page 41, and Stalin's broadcast of 1941 on page 48. Then attempt the following questions:

1. comprehension questions:
a) What reasons did Stalin give in 1931 for refusing to contemplate a slowing down of the tempo of economic development? *(5 marks)*
b) What, according to this speech, had been the main weaknesses of traditional Russia? *(6 marks)*

2. stimulus questions:
a) Explain what Stalin means by a 'scorched earth' policy (line 5, page 48). *(10 marks)*
b) Using your own knowledge, explain the differences between the 'optimal' FYP and the 'actual' FYP. *(10 marks)*

3. cross referencing question:
How far do the statistics in the table on page 41, suggest that Stalin's aims as expressed in his speech of 1931 had been achieved by the end of the First FYP? *(12 marks)*

4. source evaluation question: How valuable are the extracts from Stalin's speeches of 1931 and 1941 to the historian who is studying the motivation behind Stalin's economic policies? *(12 marks)*

5. lead-out question: In what ways do these three sources help to explain why the Soviet economy was able to survive the strains of the 1941–45 war? *(15 marks)*

4 Stalin and Political Power

POINTS TO CONSIDER

With his defeat of the Left and Right Bolsheviks, Stalin by 1929 had achieved personal power in the Soviet Union. He subsequently consolidated that power to the point of absolute control by a series of purges that continued until his death in 1953. In theory, a purge was a means of purifying and preserving the Communist Party and the Soviet State. It practice, it was the means by which Stalin destroyed or removed anyone whom he regarded as representing a threat to his authority. Your main aim in studying this chapter should be to gain an understanding of how his mastery over the machinery of Party and government enabled him to use the purge as a devastatingly effective instrument of control.

KEY DATES

1932	The trial of the Ryutin group formed the prelude to Stalin's purges.
1933	The purges began under Yezhov's direction.
1934	The assassination of Kirov provided the pretext for an intensification of the purges under Yagoda.
1935	Zhdanov, Vyshinsky and Beria took over the organising of the purges.
1941–45	The period of the 'Great Purge' of the Party, the Army and the People.
1941–45	Purges used to remove those accused of undermining the war effort.
1949	The 'Leningrad Affair' led to a further purge of the Party.
1953	The 'Doctors' Plot', which began a purge of the medical profession, was ended by the death of Stalin.

1 The Earlier Purges

> **KEY ISSUE** What form did the earlier purges take?

The Stalinist purges which began in 1933 were not unprecedented. During Lenin's time, in the early 1920s, tens of thousands of anti-Communists, variously dubbed by the authorities as 'bourgeois nationalists', 'Left-wing anti-Bolsheviks' and 'deviationists', had been imprisoned in labour camps. Public trials, such as the Shakhty affair (see page 42) had been held during the early stages of the First Five-Year Plan as a way of identifying and disgracing industrial 'saboteurs'.

However, even at this early stage, prosecutions had not been restricted to industrial enemies. In 1932 the trial of the Ryutin group had taken place. These were the followers of M.N. Ryutin, a Right Bolshevik, who had published an attack on Stalin, describing him as 'the evil genius who had brought the Revolution to the verge of destruction'. Ryutin and his supporters were publicly tried and expelled from the Party. This was the prelude to the first major purge of the CPSU by Stalin. Between 1933 and 1934 nearly one million members, over a third of the total membership, were excluded from the Party on the grounds that they were 'Ryutinites'.

At the beginning, Party purges were by no means as violent and deadly as they later became. They did not always take the form of legal proceedings; nor did they necessarily involve formal dismissal from the Party, let alone imprisonment or execution. The usual procedure was to require members to hand in their Party cards for checking, at which point any suspect individuals would not have their cards returned to them. This amounted to expulsion since, without cards, members were denied access to all Party activities. Furthermore, they and their families then found it impossible to retain employment, housing or privileged food rations. The threat of expulsion was enough to force members to conform to official Party policy. Under such a system, it became progressively difficult to mount effective opposition. Despite this, attempts were made in the early 1930s to criticise Stalin, as the Ryutin affair illustrates. These efforts were ineffectual, but they led Stalin to believe that organised resistance to him was still possible.

1934 is an important date in Stalin's rise to absolute authority. That year marks the point at which he began the systematic terrorising not of obvious political opponents but of colleagues and party members. It is difficult to explain precisely why Stalin initiated such a terror. Historians accept that they are dealing with behaviour that goes beyond reason and logic. Stalin was deeply suspicious by nature and right up to his death 20 years later he continued to believe he was under threat from actual or potential enemies. One historian, Alec Nove, offered this suggestion as to how Stalin's mind may have worked:

> 1 The revolution from above caused great hardships, coercion left many wounds. Within and outside the Party, they might dream of revenge. Party leaders rendered politically impotent might seek to exploit the situation. So: liquidate them all in good time, destroy them and their
> 5 reputations.[1]

Such thinking meant everyone was suspect; no one was safe. Purges became not so much a series of episodes as a permanent condition of Soviet political life. Terror was all-pervading. Its intensity varied from time to time, but it was an ever-present reality throughout the remainder of Stalin's life.

2 The Post-Kirov Purges, 1934–36

> **KEY ISSUE** In what sense did the post-Kirov purges mark 'Stalin's victory over the Party'?

The pretext for the purge of 1934, which set the pattern for all subsequent persecutions, was the assassination of Sergei Kirov, the secretary of the Leningrad Soviet. The strong probability is that the death-plot against Kirov had been sanctioned by Stalin himself. Nikita Khrushchev in his secret speech in 1956, which began the process of de-Stalinisation (see page 112), stated that Stalin was almost certainly behind the murder. However, a special study concluded in 1993 that while Stalin may well have been guilty, the evidence against him consists of 'unverified facts, rumours and conjectures'.[2] Yet, whatever the truth concerning Stalin's involvement, it was undeniably the case that the murder worked directly to his advantage. Kirov had been a highly popular figure in the Party. A strikingly-handsome Russian, he had made a strong impression at the 17th Party Congress in 1934 and had been elected to the Politburo. He was known to be unhappy with the speed and scale of Stalin's industrialisation drive. He was also opposed to extreme measures being used as a means of disciplining Party members. If organised opposition to Stalin were to form within the Party, Kirov was an outstanding example of the type of individual around whom dissatisfied Party members might rally.

Stalin was quick to exploit the opportunity the assassination provided. Under the guise of exacting retribution for the murder, a fresh purge of the Party was begun. Stalin claimed that Kirov's death had been organised by a wide circle of Trotskyites and Leftists, who must all be brought to account. There followed a large-scale round-up of the suspected conspirators, who were then imprisoned or executed. The atmosphere was captured in an account by Victor Serge, one of the 'oppositionists' who managed to flee from the USSR at this time:

> 1   I am convinced that at the end of 1934, just at the moment when Kirov
> was murdered, the Politburo was entering upon a policy of normality
> and relaxation. The shot fired by Nikolayev [the assassin] ushered in an
> era of panic and savagery. The immediate response was the execution
> 5   of 114 people, then the execution of Nikolayev and his friends; then the
> arrest and imprisonment of the whole of the former Zinoviev and
> Kamenev tendency, close on 3,000 persons, as far as I could make out;
> then the mass deportation of tens of thousands of Leningrad citizens,
> simultaneously with hundreds of arrests among those already deported
> 10   and the opening of fresh secret trials in the prisons. On Nikolayev's
> crime, the world has seen the publication of a number of successive versions, all of them lavish in improbabilities, but not of the original papers,
> whether the terrorists' own statements or the documents of the inves-

tigation. It was almost certainly an individual act committed by an
15 enraged Communist. The Left or Trotskyite Opposition had nothing
whatever to do with the assassination.[3]

It is an interesting coincidence that just as Stalin's path to power had
been smoothed ten years earlier by 'the Lenin enrolment' (see page
13), so in 1934 his successful purge had been made a great deal easier
by a recent major shift in the composition of the Party. During the
previous three years the CPSU had recruited into its ranks a higher
proportion of skilled workers and industrial managers than at any
time since 1917. Stalin encouraged this as a means of tightening the
links between the Party and those actually operating the First Five-
Year Plan, but it also had the result of introducing into the CPSU a
considerable number of members who joined the Party primarily to
advance their careers. Acutely aware that their newly acquired privileges were a direct consequence of Stalin's patronage, such members
willingly supported the elimination of the anti-Stalinist elements in
the Party. After all, it improved their own chances of promotion. The
competition for jobs in Soviet Russia was invariably fierce. Purges
always left positions to be filled. As the chief dispenser of positions,
Stalin knew that the self-interest of these new Party members would
keep them loyal to him. Norman Stone, a Western analyst of the
Soviet Union, used a memorable simile to describe this: 'It was characteristic of Stalin to have his own allies "marked" by their own subordinates: in Stalin's system identical thugs kept on replacing each
other, like so many Russian dolls'.

The preliminary purge in 1933 was arranged by Yezhov, the poi-
sonous chief of the Control Commission, the branch of the Central
Committee responsible for Party discipline. The full-scale purge that
followed Kirov's murder in 1934 was the work of Yagoda, head of the
newly-formed NKVD, which had superseded the OGPU in that year as
the State security force. In 1935 Kirov's key post as Party boss in
Leningrad was filled by Zhdanov, described by one contemporary
Communist, who managed to escape the purges, as 'a toady without
an idea in his head'. The equivalent position in Moscow was filled by
another ardent Stalinist, Nikita Khrushchev. In recognition of his strident courtroom bullying of 'oppositionists' in the earlier purge trials,
Andrei Vyshinsky, a reformed Menshevik, was appointed State
Prosecutor.

Stalin's fellow-Georgian, Lavrenti Beria, was entrusted with over-
seeing State security in the national-minority areas of the USSR. With
another of Stalin's protégés, Poskrebyshev, in charge of the
Secretariat, there was no significant area of the Soviet bureaucracy
which Stalin did not control. Public or Party opinion meant nothing
when set against Stalin's grip on the key personnel and functions in
Party and government. There had been rumours, around the time of
the second FYP, of a possible move to oust him from the position of

Secretary General. These were silenced in the aftermath of the Kirov affair.

The outstanding feature of the post-Kirov purge was the status of many of its victims. Prominent among those arrested were Kamenev and Zinoviev, who, along with Stalin, had formed the triumvirate after Lenin's death in 1924 and who had been the leading Left Bolsheviks in the power struggle of the 1920s. At the time of their arrest in 1935 they were not accused of involvement in Kirov's assassination, only of having engaged in 'opposition', a charge that had no precise meaning. However, the significance of their arrest and imprisonment was plain to all: no Party members, whatever their rank or revolutionary pedigree, were safe.

What gave Yagoda and the operators of the purge such sweeping powers was the government's 'decree against terrorist acts', issued after Kirov's murder, which made the NKVD a law unto itself in pursuing the enemies of the State and the Party. Arbitrary arrest and summary execution became the norm. In the post-Stalin years it was admitted by Khrushchev that the decree had become the justification for 'broad acts which contravened socialist justice', a euphemism for mass murder. An impression of this can be gained from glancing at the fate of the representatives at the party Congress of 1934. Of the 1,996 delegates who attended, 1,108 were executed during the next three years. In addition, out of the 139 Central Committee members elected at that gathering all but 41 of them were put to death during the purges. Leonard Shapiro, in his study of the CPSU, described these events as 'Stalin's victory over the Party'. From this point on, the Soviet Communist Party was entirely under his control. It ceased, in effect, to have a separate existence. Stalin had become the Party.

3 The Great Purge, 1936–39

> **KEY ISSUE** Was there any logic to the Great Purge?

It might be expected that once Stalin's absolute supremacy over the Party had been established the purges would stop. But they increased in intensity. Stalin declared that the Soviet Union was in 'a state of siege' and called for still greater vigilance in unmasking the enemies within. In 1936 a progressive terrorising of the Soviet Union began which affected the entire population, but took its most dramatic form in the public show trials of Stalin's former Bolshevik colleagues. The one-time heroes of the 1917 Revolution and the Civil War were arrested, tried and executed as enemies of the state. Remarkably, the great majority went to their death after confessing their guilt and accepting the truth of the charges levelled against them. Such was the scale of the persecution at this time, and so high ranking were the victims, that it has gone down in history as 'the Great Purge'.

The descriptions applied to the accused during the purges bore little relation to political reality. 'Right', 'Left' and Centre' opposition blocs were identified and the groupings invariably had the catch-all term 'Trotskyite' tagged on to them, but such words were convenient prosecution labels rather than definitions of a genuine political opposition. They were the preliminary means of isolating those in the Communist Party and the Soviet State whom Stalin wished to destroy.

a) The Purge of the Party

There is a similarity between the purges of the 1930s and the post-Lenin power struggle of a decade earlier. In each case it was the Left who first came under attack, followed by an assault on the Right. The prelude to the Great Purge of 1936 was a secret letter sent from CPSU headquarters, warning all the local Party branches of a terrorist conspiracy by 'the Trotskyite–Kamenevite–Zinovievite–Leftist Counter-Revolutionary Bloc' and instructing Party officials to begin rooting out suspected agents and sympathisers. Once this campaign of denunciation and expulsion had been set in motion in the country at large, Kamenev and Zinoviev were put on public trial in Moscow, charged with involvement in Kirov's murder and with plotting to overthrow the Soviet State. Both men pleaded guilty and read their abject written confessions in court. The obvious question is 'Why did they confess?' After all, these men were tough Bolsheviks. No doubt, as was later revealed during de-Stalinisation, physical and psychological torture was used. Possibly more important was their sense of demoralisation at having been accused and disgraced by the Party which could do no wrong and to which they had dedicated their lives. In a curious sense, their admission of guilt was a last act of loyalty to the Party.

Whatever their reasons, and these continue to be a puzzle to historians, the fact that they did confess made it extremely difficult for other victims of the purges to plead their own innocence. If the great ones of State and party were prepared to accept their fate, on what grounds could lesser men resist? The psychological impact of the public confessions of such figures as Kamenev and Zinoviev was profound. It helped to create an atmosphere in which innocent victims cravenly submitted in open court to false charges, and went to their death begging the Party's forgiveness. It also shows Stalin's astuteness in insisting on a policy of public trials. There is little doubt that Stalin had the power to conduct the purges without using legal proceedings. However, by making the victims deliver humiliating confessions while on public trial, he was able to reveal the scale of the conspiracy against him and to prove the need for the purging to continue. There was also a political bonus in that the victims' confessions invariably incriminated others, thereby easing the task of further detection and justifying the continuation of harsh measures.

This soon became evident after Kamenev and Zinoviev, along with 14 other Bolsheviks, had been duly executed in keeping with Vyshinsky's notorious demand as Prosecutor that they be shot 'like the mad dogs they are'. The details that the condemned had revealed in their confessions were used to prepare the next major strike, the attack upon 'the Right deviationists'. Bukharin, Rykov and Tomsky were put under investigation, but not yet formally charged. The delay was caused by the reluctance of some of the older Bolsheviks in the Politburo to denounce their comrades. Stalin intervened personally to speed up the process. Yagoda, who was considered to have shown too much sensitivity in his recent handling of the 'Trotskyite-Zinovievite bloc', was replaced as head of the NKVD by the less scrupulous Yezhov whose name, like Vyshinsky's, was to become a byword for terror.

Meanwhile, the case for proceeding against Bukharin and the Right was strengthened by the revelations at a further show trial in 1937, at which 17 Communists, denounced collectively as the 'Anti-Soviet Trotskyist Centre', were charged with spying for Nazi Germany. The accused included Radek and Pyatakov, the former favourites of Lenin, and Sokolnikov, Stalin's Commissar for Finance during the First FYP. Radek's grovelling confession in which he incriminated his close colleagues, including his friend Bukharin, saved him from the death sentence imposed on all but three of the other defendants. (He died two years later in an Arctic labour camp.) Yezhov and Vyshinsky now had the evidence they needed. In 1938, in the third of the major show trials, Bukharin and Rykov (Tomsky had taken his own life in the meantime) and 18 other 'Trotskyite-Rightists' were publicly arraigned on a variety of counts, including sabotage, spying and conspiracy to murder Stalin. The fact that Yagoda was one of the accused was a sign of the speed with which the terror was starting to consume its own kind. Fitzroy MacLean, a British diplomat, was one of the foreign contingent permitted to observe the trial. His description conveys the character of the proceedings:

1   It was an impressive list [of defendants]: Bukharin, a former Secretary-General of the Communist International, for years the leading theorist of the Party and a close associate of Lenin; Rykov, Lenin's successor and Molotov's predecessor as Premier; Yagoda who, until eighteen months
5   ago, had been People's Commissar for Internal Affairs and supreme head of the all-powerful NKVD.
    The prisoners were charged, collectively and individually, with every conceivable crime: high treason, murder, espionage and all kinds of sabotage. They had plotted to wreck industry and agriculture, to assassi-
10 nate Stalin, to dismember the Soviet Union for the benefit of their capitalist allies. They were shown for the most part to have been criminals and traitors to the Soviet cause ever since the Revolution – before it even. The evidence accumulated filled no less than fifty large volumes.

One after another, using the same words, they admitted their guilt:
15 Bukharin, Rykov, Yagoda. Each prisoner incriminated his fellows and
was in turn incriminated by them. There was no attempt to evade
responsibility. They were men in full possession of their faculties; the
statements they made were closely reasoned and delivered with every
appearance of spontaneity. And yet what they said, the actual contents
20 of their statements seemed, to bear no relation to reality.

As the trial progressed, it became ever clearer that the underlying
purpose of every testimony was to blacken the leaders of the 'bloc', to
represent them, not as political offenders, but as common criminals,
murderers, poisoners and spies.[4]

At one point in the trial Bukharin embarrassed the court by attempting to defend himself, but he was eventually silenced by Vyshinsky's
bullying and was sentenced to be shot along with the rest of the defendants. In his final speech in court Bukharin showed the extraordinary
character of the Bolshevik mentality. Despite the injustice of the proceedings to which he had been subjected, he accepted the infallibility
of the Party and of Stalin:

1 When you ask yourself: 'If you must die, what are you dying for?' – an
absolutely black vacuity suddenly rises before you with starling vivid-
ness. There was nothing to die for, if one wanted to die unrepented.
And, on the contrary, everything positive that glistens in the Soviet
5 Union acquires new dimensions in a man's mind. This in the end dis-
armed me completely and led me to bend my knees before the Party
and the country ... For in reality the whole country stands behind
Stalin; he is the hope of the world.[5]

A particular irony attached to Bukharin's execution. Only two years
previously he had been the principal draftsman of the new constitution of the USSR. This 1936 Constitution, which Stalin described as
'the most democratic in the world', was intended to impress Western
Communists and Soviet sympathisers with the legal propriety of the
USSR. This was the period in Soviet foreign policy when, in an effort
to offset the Nazi menace to the USSR, Stalin was urging the formation of 'popular fronts' between the Communist parties and the various Left-wing groups in Europe (see page 84). In addition to defining
the relationship between the independent federal Republics of the
USSR, the 1936 Constitution claimed that socialism had been established and that there were no longer any 'classes' in Soviet society; all
exploitation having ended, there were now only 'strata' of workers
and peasants, working in harmony for the mutual good of all. The
basic civil rights of freedom of expression, assembly, and worship
were guaranteed.

However, the true character of Stalin's Constitution lay not in what
it said but in what it omitted to say. Hardly anywhere was the role of
the Party mentioned; its powers were not defined and, therefore, were
not curtailed. It would remain the instrument through which Stalin

would exercise his total control of the USSR. It is possible to argue that nowhere was the fraudulent nature of Stalinism as a system of government more clearly evident than in the Constitution of 1936. It was issued when the purges were at their height. The contrast between its democratic claims and the reality of the situation in the Soviet Union could not have been greater.

b) The Purge of the Army

The targets of the purges were not restricted to Party members and government officials. A significant development occurred in 1937 when the Soviet military came under threat. Stalin's control of the Soviet Union would not have been complete if the armed services had continued as an independent force. It was essential that they be kept subservient. Knowing that military loyalties might make a purge of the army difficult to achieve, Stalin took the preliminary step of organising a large number of transfers within the higher ranks in order to lessen the possibility of centres of resistance being formed when the attack came.

With this accomplished, Vyshinksy announced, in May 1937, that 'a gigantic conspiracy' had been uncovered in the Red Army. Marshal Tukhachevsky, the popular and talented Chief of General Staff, was arrested along with seven other generals, all of whom had been 'heroes of the Civil War'. On the grounds that speed was essential to prevent a military coup, the trial was held immediately and in secret. The charge was treason; Tukhachevsky was accused of having spied for Germany and Japan. Documentary evidence, some of it supplied by German intelligence at the request of the NKVD, was produced in proof. The outcome was predetermined and inevitable. In June 1937 after their ritual confession and condemnation Tukhachevsky and his fellow generals were shot. There appears to have been a particularly personal element in all this. The President of the secret court which delivered the death sentences was Marshal Voroshilov, a devoted Stalinist, who had long been jealous of Tukhachevsky's superior abilities and greater popularity.

Tukhachevsky's execution was the signal for an even greater bloodletting. To prevent any chance of a military reaction, a wholesale destruction of the Red Army establishment was undertaken. In the following 18 months all 11 War Commissars were removed from office; three of the five Marshals of the Soviet Union were dismissed; 75 of the 80-man Supreme Military Council were executed; 14 of the 16 army commanders, and nearly two-thirds of the 280 divisional commanders, were removed; half of the commissioned officer corps, 35,000 in total, were either imprisoned or shot. It was reported that in some army camps at the height of the purge officers were taken away in lorry loads for execution. The Soviet Navy was also purged; all the serving admirals of the fleet were shot and thousands of naval officers

This montage, composed by Trotsky's supporters, points to the remarkable fact that of the original 1917 Central Committee of the Bolshevik Party only Stalin was still alive in 1938. The majority of the other 23 members had, of course, been destroyed in the purges.

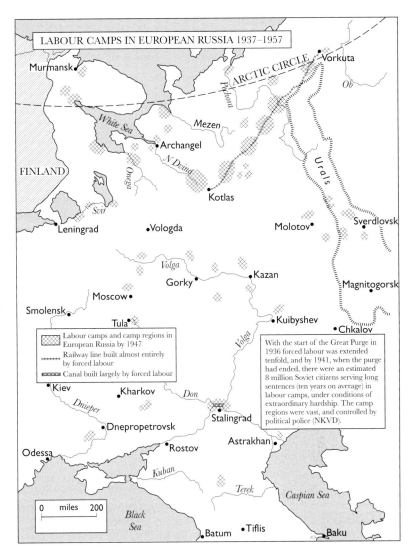

LABOUR CAMPS IN EUROPEAN RUSSIA 1937–1957

Murmansk

ARCTIC CIRCLE Vorkuta

Pechora *Ob*

White Sea Mezen

Archangel

FINLAND *N Dvina*

Onega

Kotlas

Svir Molotov Sverdlovsk

Leningrad Vologda

Volga Kazan Magnitogorsk

Gorky

Moscow

Smolensk Kuibyshev

Tula Chkalov

Labour camps and camp regions in
European Russia by 1947

Railway line built almost entirely
by forced labour

Canal built largely by forced labour

Volga

With the start of the Great Purge in
1936 forced labour was extended
tenfold, and by 1941, when the purge
had ended, there were an estimated
8 million Soviet citizens serving long
sentences (ten years on average) in
labour camps, under conditions of
extraordinary hardship. The camp
regions were vast, and controlled by
political police (NKVD).

Kiev Kharkov *Don*

Dnieper

Dnepropetrovsk Stalingrad

Astrakhan

Odessa Rostov

Kuban

Terek *Caspian Sea*

0 miles 200

*Black
Sea* Batum Tiflis Baku

By 1941, as a result of the purges, there were an estimated eight million
prisoners in the camps. The average sentence was ten years, which, given
the terrible conditions in the camps, was equivalent to a death sentence.

were imprisoned in labour camps. The Soviet Air Force was similarly
decimated, only one of its senior commanders surviving the purge.

The devastation of the Soviet armed forces, wholly unrelated to any
conceivable military purpose, was complete by 1939. It left all three
services seriously undermanned and staffed by inexperienced or
incompetent replacements. Given the defence needs of the USSR, a

theme constantly stressed by Stalin himself, the deliberate crippling of the Soviet military is the aspect of the purges that most defies logic. It is the strongest evidence in support of the contention that Stalin had lost touch with reality.

c) The Purge of the People

Stalin's achievement of total dominance over Party, government, and military did not mean the end of the purges. The apparatus of terror was retained and the search for enemies continued. Purges were used to achieve the goals of the FYPs; charges of industrial sabotage were made against managers and workers in the factories. The purge was also a way of forcing the regions and nationalities into total subordination to Stalin. The show trials that had taken place in Moscow and Leningrad, with their catalogue of accusations, confessions, and death sentences, were copied in all the republics of the USSR. The terror they created was no less intense for being localised. For example, between 1937 and 1939 in Stalin's home state of Georgia, two state prime ministers were removed, four-fifths of the regional Party secretaries and thousands of lesser officials lost their posts. This was accompanied by a wide-ranging purge of the legal and academic professions. Foreign Communists living in the Soviet Union were not immune. Polish and German revolutionary exiles were rounded up in scores, and many of them were imprisoned or executed. The outstanding foreign victim was Bela Kun, the leader of the short-lived Communist revolution in Hungary in 1919. He was condemned and shot in 1936.

No area of Soviet life escaped being purged. The constant fear that this created conditioned the whole Soviet people. Under Stalin terror was elevated into a method of government. Understandably, historians tend to concentrate on the central and dramatic features of the purges, such as the show trials and the attack upon the Party and the Red Army, but the greatest impact of the purges in terms of aggregate numbers was on the middle and lower ranks of Soviet society. One in 18 of the population were arrested during Stalin's purges. Almost every family in the USSR suffered the loss of at least one of its members as a victim of the terror.

In the headlong rush to uncover more and more conspiracies, to search out more and more culprits, interrogators themselves became victims and joined those they had condemned in execution cells and labour camps. Concepts such as innocence and guilt, truth and falsehood, seemed to lose all meaning during the purges. The mass of the population were frightened and bewildered. Fear had the effect of destroying moral values and traditional loyalties. The one aim was survival, even at the cost of betrayal. In an edition devoted to a study of the Stalinist purges, the Moscow *Literary Gazette* spoke in 1988 of 'the special sadism, the sophisticated barbarism, whereby the nearest relatives were forced to incriminate each other – brother to slander brother, husband to blacken wife'. The chillingly systematic character of the purges was described in the minutes of a plenary session of the Central Committee, held in June 1957 during the de-Stalinisation period (see page 112).

1 Between 27 February 1937 and 12 November 1938 the NKVD received
approval from Stalin, Molotov and Kagonovich for the Military
Collegium and Supreme court to sentence to death by shooting 38,697.
On one day, 12 November 1938, Stalin and Molotov sanctioned the
5 execution of 3,167 people. On 21 November the NKVD received
approval from Stalin and Molotov to shoot 229 people, including
twenty-three members and candidate members of the Central
Committee, twenty-two members of the Party Control Commission,
twelve regional Party secretaries, twenty-one People's Commissars,
10 136 commissariat officials and fifteen military personnel.[6]

4 The Later Purges, 1941–53

> **KEY ISSUE** Did the continuation of the purges after 1941 indicate
> they had become an integral part of the Stalinist system of
> government?

The purges continued into wartime. Stalin blamed military failures on internal sabotage and persecuted those deemed responsible. Neither the war nor its outcome lessened his vindictiveness. He emerged from the war harder in attitude towards the Soviet people, despite their heroic efforts, and more suspicious of the outside world, despite the alliances entered into by the USSR. The undeniable fact that many Soviet troops had deserted to the enemy, particularly in the early phases of the war, provided the justification for a large-scale purge of the Soviet armed forces at the end of the war. At the Yalta and Potsdam Conferences in 1945 the Allies had agreed in principle that all released prisoners-of-war should be returned to their country of origin. In central and eastern Europe these included many Soviet citizens who had fought for Germany against the USSR in an attempt to break free of Stalin. Not unnaturally, they were terrified at the prospect of what awaited them and pleaded with their Allied captors not to be sent back. However, in the face of Stalin's insistence, the Allies gave in and forcibly repatriated the prisoners they held.

The consequences were as appalling as the prisoners had anticipated. Mass executions took place on Stalin's orders. What deepened the tragedy was that the victims were not only fighting-men. On the grounds that whole communities had supported Hitler's forces, whole communities were made to suffer. It was at this time that the Cossacks as a people were virtually destroyed, as a punishment for

Stalin signing an order for the execution of 6,600 condemned prisoners. An interesting point of comparison is that this number exceeded that of all those executed for political offences in tsarist Russia in the one hundred years up to 1917.

their support of the German armies during the war. Stalin was no gentler to the Soviet POWs who returned from German captivity. He did not disguise his contempt for them, apparently believing that their very survival somehow indicated that they had collaborated with their captors. It was not uncommon in 1945 for prisoners to be released from German prison camps, only to be transferred directly into Soviet labour camps. Their callous treatment at his hands was further evidence that the purges would continue. The USSR's victory in the Great Patriotic War had not deflected Stalin from his policy of exacting absolute obedience from the Soviet people. The camps would remain. There would be the same unrelenting search for victims to fill them.

His suspicion of the hostile designs of the West on the USSR, which had been deepened rather than diminished by his wartime contacts with Allied leaders, led him to demand that still greater attention be given to state security. The westward push of the Red Army during the final stages of the war had left the USSR in occupation of large areas of central Europe. In one obvious sense this greatly added to Soviet strength. But Stalin's determination at the end of the war to cling on to these regions and turn them into satellites created its own difficulties. It increased Cold War tensions between East and West and it widened the area of Soviet security fears. To balance this, Stalin insisted that the governments of the new Soviet bloc give priority to suppressing all forms of opposition to themselves and to the Soviet Union. The methods by which Stalin's Russia had been ruled during the previous 15 years became (with the single exception of Yugoslavia) the norm in the satellites. The national Communist Party, totally loyal to Stalin and the USSR and kept so by frequent purges, governed in each of the countries of the Soviet bloc. The sycophantic daily adulation of Stalin in the Soviet press was repeated in all the satellites. Stalin's was the living and unchallengeable voice of international Marxism-Leninism.

Such acclaim in no way lessened the rigidity of Stalin's outlook. Indeed, as he grew older he became more critical and suspicious of those around him. After 1947 he dispensed with the Central Committee and the Politburo, thus removing even the semblance of limitation upon his authority. In 1949 he initiated another Party purge, 'the Leningrad Affair', comparable in scale and style to those of the 1930s. Leading Party and city officials, including those who had previously been awarded the title 'Hero of the Soviet Union' in honour of their courageous defence of Leningrad during the war, were arrested, tried on charges of attempting to use Leningrad as an opposition base, and shot.

Soviet Jews were the next section of the population to be purged. Stalin ordered what amounted to a pogrom for no better reason than that his daughter, Alliluyeva, had had an affair with a Jew of whom he disapproved. Anti-Semitism was a long-established tradition in Russia and it was a factor in the last purge Stalin attempted. Early in 1953 it was officially announced from the Kremlin that a 'Doctors' Plot' had been uncovered in Moscow; it was asserted that the Jewish-dominated medical centre had planned to murder Stalin and the other Soviet leaders. Preparations began for a major assault on the Soviet medical profession, comparable to the pre-war devastation of the Red Army. What prevented those preparations being put into operation was the death of Stalin in March 1953.

5 The Purges in Perspective

> **KEY ISSUES** Why was there so little resistance to the purges in the Soviet Union?
> How far beyond Stalin did the responsibility for the purges extend?

It is still not possible for historians to give a precise figure of those destroyed during Stalin's purges. However, in the 1990s limited access to the files of the KGB was granted to scholars. The following represent some of the most reliable figures now available:

> In **1934**, one million were arrested and executed in the first major purge, mainly in Moscow and Leningrad.
> By **1937**, 17 to 18 million had been transported to labour camps; 10 million of these died.
> By **1939**, another five to seven million had been 'repressed', one million of these being shot, another one to two million dying in the camps.
> In **1940**, the occupation of the Baltic states (Lithuania, Estonia and Latvia), Bukovina and Bessarabia resulted in two million being deported, most of whom died.
> In **1941**, the deportation to Siberia of various national groups, including Germans, Kalmyks, Ukrainians, Chechens and Crimean Tatars, led to the deaths of one third of the four million involved.
> Between **1944** and **1946**, the 'screening' of returned prisoners of war and those who had been under German occupation resulted in 10 million being transported to the labour camps of the gulag; five to six million of these died in captivity.
> Between **1947** and **1953**, one million died in the various purges and repressions during the last six years of Stalin's life.

A grim reflection is that in the sheer scale of its misery and death the Stalinist repression of the Soviet peoples outweighed even the holocaust, the Nazi genocide of six million Jews in occupied Europe. Only a partial answer can be offered as to why Stalin engaged for so long in such a destructive exercise. One motive was obviously the desire to impose his absolute authority by bringing all the organs of Party and State under his control. Yet even after that aim had been achieved the terror continued. The purges were so excessive and gratuitously brutal that they defy logical analysis. His suspicions and fears revealed a deep irrationality amounting to paranoia. That, indeed, was how his daughter, Alliluyeva, saw it:

1   As he'd got older my father had begun feeling lonely. He was so isolated from everyone that he seemed to be living in a vacuum. He hadn't a soul he could talk to. It was the system of which he himself was the prisoner and in which he was stifling from emptiness and lack of human com-
5 panionship.[7]

Psychology is a difficult area of historical research; it is not easy to judge an individual's mental processes. Nonetheless, Stalin's behaviour was so unbalanced that it casts doubt on his sanity. Robert Conquest, an outstanding Western historian of the purges, found Stalin's conduct to have been so contrary to the USSR's real needs as to be inexplicable in rational terms. Nor was that just the view of a Western liberal. In the freer atmosphere of the 1990s, Russian writers began to acknowledge the enormity of Stalin's campaigns of terror. In Dmitri Volkogonov's estimation (which does not include the ten million war dead), 'Between 1929 and 1953 the state created by Lenin and set in motion by Stalin deprived 21.5 million Soviet citizens of their lives. No one in history has ever waged such war on his own people.'

When due allowance has been made for the mental and physical pressures applied to the accused, it has still to be explained why the great majority succumbed with so little resistance. Torture and coercion were not the whole story. We have to remember the role that the Party played in the lives of the Bolshevik old-guard. Most of the new recruits may have been time-servers and careerists, but, for the old Bolsheviks of 1917 and the Civil War years, membership of the CPSU was not merely a matter of political affiliation – it was a way of life. In medieval Christendom there was a saying 'Outside the Church there is no salvation'. That dogma may be suitably adapted to describe the attitude of the traditional Bolsheviks: 'outside the Party life has no purpose'. It was their very dedication to the Party that led them to accept their fate. As individuals they knew they were innocent of the charges, but what did individuality matter when set against the collective truth of the Party? The Party's infallibility persuaded the condemned to accept the justice of the verdicts imposed on them. One of the old Bolsheviks, Yorykin, despite having been falsely charged, tortured and condemned, despite having seen his wife abused and his family deported, all on the personal orders of Stalin, could still cry out in the final seconds before he was shot 'Long live the Party, long live Comrade Stalin!' The Bolshevik mentality often baffles the judgement of the neutral historian, but there is enough evidence in the writings of Stalin's victims to indicate the peculiar power that the concept of Bolshevik loyalty exercised over the minds of Party members. Of course, not all the accused thought in this way. Many were helpless victims of what became a mass hysteria, which paralysed all thought of resistance and led individuals to try to escape by incriminating others. In such an atmosphere, in which guilt not innocence was assumed, an accusation was tantamount to proof.

While fully accepting that Stalin was the architect of the terror, historians have begun to look beyond him in assessing the responsibility for the purges. Their approach has been prompted by their reading of Russian archival material that shows that Stalinism was not as monolithic a system of government as has been traditionally assumed. Attention has shifted to the disorganised state of much of Soviet bureaucracy, particularly at local level. The purges were clearly initiated by Stalin himself, but how they were actually carried out largely depended on the local Party organisation. It is arguable that the fragmentation and disruption of Soviet society, caused by the massive upheavals of collectivisation and industrialisation, destroyed any semblance of social stability and so encouraged Party and government officials to resort to the most extreme measures. An insight into the Russian mind-set that permitted all this to happen is offered by a Russian writer:

1 People like Stalin regard conscience as a chimera [a myth]. One cannot speak of the conscience of a dictator; he simply did not have one. The people who did his dirty deeds for him, however, knew full well what they were doing. In such people conscience had 'gone cold'. In conse-
5 quence, the people allowed their own consciences to be driven into a reservation, thus giving the grand inquisitor the authority to carry on with his dark deeds.[8]

In this connection, an interesting interpretation has been advanced by a number of modern scholars, among whom J. Arch Getty is the most prominent, which argues that the purges came from below as much as from above. According to this view, the purges begun by Stalin were sustained in their ferocity by the lower rank officials in government and party eager to replace their superiors, whom they regarded as a conservative elite. Thus the dynamic of the purges was provided by the ruthless ambition of those on the lower rungs of the Party who were seeking preferment and position. It was certainly true that Stalin had no difficulty in finding eager subordinates to organise the purges. The common characteristic of those who led Stalin's campaigns was their unswerving personal loyalty to him, a loyalty that overcame any scruples they might have had regarding the nature of their work. They were an unsavoury group of individuals whose marked lack of cultural refinement or moral sensibility added to the detestation and terror in which they were held by their victims.

References

1   Alec Nove, *Stalinism and After* (Unwin Hyman, 1975).
2   J. Arch Getty and R. T. Manning, *Stalinist Terror: New Perspectives* (Cambridge, 1993), p.47.
3   Victor Serge, *Memoirs of a Revolutionary, 1901–41*, (OUP, 1963), pp.313–14.
4   Fitzroy MacClean, *Eastern Approaches,* (Jonathan Cape, 1951).
5   Quoted in Piers Brendon, *The Dark Valley: A Panorama of the 1930s* (Jonathan Cape, 2000), p.569.
6   From the Russian Presidential Archives, quoted in Dmitri Volkogonov, *The Rise and Fall of the Soviet Empire: Political Leaders from Lenin to Gorbachev* (HarperCollins, 1998), p.250.
7   Svetlana Alliluyeva, *Twenty letters to a Friend* (Penguin, 1968), p.106.
8   Dmitri Volkogonov, *Stalin Triumph and Tragedy* (Weidenfeld and Nicolson, 1991), pp.580–81.

Summary
'Stalin and Power'

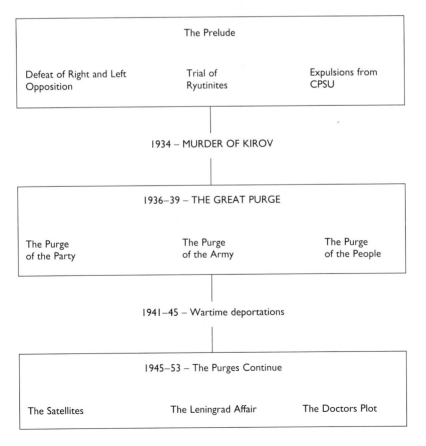

The Prelude

| Defeat of Right and Left Opposition | Trial of Ryutinites | Expulsions from CPSU |

1934 – MURDER OF KIROV

1936–39 – THE GREAT PURGE

| The Purge of the Party | The Purge of the Army | The Purge of the People |

1941–45 – Wartime deportations

1945–53 – The Purges Continue

| The Satellites | The Leningrad Affair | The Doctors Plot |

Working on Chapter 4

Your aim should be to understand the way in which Stalin used the power which he held from the late 1920s onwards to destroy all sources of opposition to him. Although the purges may be thought of as forming a single system of oppression, it is important that you note the differences between them. Use the section headings and Key Issues to assist you in this. There are three fundamental issues in regard to Stalin's use of power, to which almost all other questions relate:

(a) What were Stalin's motives?
(b) By what means did he seek to achieve his aims?
(c) Why was there no effective resistance to him?

In responding to the first question you need to examine his aims as Soviet leader. This in turn leads to an analysis of the ways he put those aims into practice. In looking at those ways you become involved in studying why his methods were accepted and his orders obeyed. Put in very simple terms, you are asking: What did Stalin want to do? How did he go about it? How did he get away with it? If you shape your study around these three questions you are unlikely to ignore anything of real importance.

Answering structured and essay questions on Chapter 4

The following questions relate to each of the five main sections of this chapter. Notice that the a) questions are the more direct type, asking for a description of events, while the b) questions are more demanding since they call for analysis and judgement.

1. a) In what ways had purges been used before 1934 to enforce Party loyalty?
 b) Explain the importance of the trial of the Ryuntinites in 1932 as a stage in the development of the Stalinist purges.
2. a) Describe the ways in which 'the Lenin enrolment' worked to Stalin's advantage in the aftermath of Kirov's assassination
 b) Explain the political significance of the Kirov murder in 1934.
3. a) Trace the main steps in the development of the Great Purge of 1936–39.
 b) How far do you agree that 'the purges strengthened Stalin personally, but weakened the Soviet Union nationally'?
4. a) In what ways did Stalin adjust the purge system to meet his perception of the USSR's needs during and after the war of 1941–45?
 b) Did the post-1945 Stalin purges serve any real Soviet interest?
5. a) Trace the statistical record of Stalin's repression of the Soviet people between 1932 and 1953.

b) 'The real puzzle is not why Stalin conducted a policy of terror, but why the Soviet Union accepted it.' How acceptable do you find this view?

Consider question 2b. It is best to begin by drawing up a list of all the relevant points. These should include details of the political situation before the assassination, of the murder itself and of Stalin's reaction to it. Having drawn up your list, you should then begin to shape the points into an essay framework. Your opening paragraph should explain briefly how far Stalin had established his authority over the Party by 1934. The second paragraph should describe Kirov's standing in the Party and should suggest why Stalin saw this as a threat. A further short paragraph, describing what is known of the murder and Stalin's probable collusion in it, would be an appropriate lead-in to Stalin's public response to it. You are now in a position to explain, in two or three paragraphs, how Stalin used Kirov's assassination as a pretext to justify a wide-ranging and sustained purge of the Party, which became the pattern for all the subsequent purges. To give weight to your argument you should refer to the Great Purge of 1936–39. Your conclusion should emphasise the key points you have made, particular stress being laid on the murder being used as the justification for the extension of the purges of the CPSU.

Source-based questions on Chapter 4

Re-read Victor Serge's account (page 57), Fitzroy MacLean's description (page 61), and Dmitri Volkogonov's comment (page 72)

1. comprehension questions:
a) According to Serge, what impact did the assassination of Kirov in 1934 have on political attitudes at the time? *(5 marks)*
b) From MacLean's eye-witness account, what can you learn about the procedures adopted at the show trials? *(8 marks)*
2. stimulus question: Using your own knowledge, suggest likely reasons for Stalin's attending as a mourner at Kirov's funeral. *(10 marks)*
3. cross referencing question: How far do the three sources agree in their depiction of the atmosphere prevailing in the USSR during the period of the Stalinist purges? *(12 marks)*
4. source evaluation questions:
a) How reliable would you judge Serge's description to be as an analysis of the reasons for Kirov's murder? *(10 marks)*
b) How valuable are these three sources to the historian who is studying the character of Stalin's leadership of the USSR between 1939 and 1953? *(12 marks)*
5. lead-out question: How do these sources help to explain why Stalin met such little resistance to the purges? *(15 marks)*

5 Stalin and International Relations

POINTS TO CONSIDER

The Soviet Union's foreign relations were of enormous importance in the history of the twentieth century. Stalin was a central figure in all this. The policies he pursued helped to shape the international scene for the greater part of the century. To help you understand his impact, this chapter begins by analysing Soviet foreign policy between the 1917 Revolution and Stalin's coming to power in the late 1920s. It was during that period that the Bolsheviks reluctantly realised that the world revolution which they had expected to follow their 1917 rising would not in fact take place. Stalin accepted the reality of this situation and for the rest of his career adopted an essentially defensive attitude towards the outside world. This explains the apparent twists and turns of Soviet foreign policy under him, which are analysed in the succeeding sections.

KEY DATES

1918–20	Foreign invasions of Russia during the Civil War.
1919	Communist International (Comintern) established.
1920	Red Army invaded Poland but was driven out.
1921	Anglo-Soviet Trade Agreement.
1922	Treaty of Rapallo signed between Soviet Russia and Germany.
1924	Anglo-Soviet relations soured by the Zinoviev Letter.
1925	Stalin suspicious of the Locarno Pact.
1926	Britain accused Soviet Union of abetting the General Strike.
1927	Stalin supported the opponents of the Chinese Communist Party; Russia feared a joint attack from the western capitalist countries.
1929	Britain formally recognised the USSR.
1933–39	Nazi Germany a constant threat to Soviet security.
1934	USSR admitted to the League of Nations.
1935	Defensive agreement between USSR, France and Czechoslovakia; Stalin encouraged European Communists to form 'popular fronts' with non-Marxist left-wing parties against fascism.
1936	The Anti-Comintern Pact signed by Germany, Italy and Japan.
1936–39	Soviet Union involved in the Spanish Civil War.
1938	The Munich Agreement appeared to isolate the USSR.
1939	The Nazi-Soviet Pact allowed Germany and USSR to carve up Poland.
1941	Hitler unleashed Operation Barbarossa against Soviet Union.
1941–45	USSR allied with USA and Britain in the Grand Alliance.

1945   The Yalta and Potsdam Conferences revealed the deep
          differences between the Soviet Union and its former allies.
1947   The Truman Doctrine and the Marshall Plan seen by Stalin as
          Western aggression against the Soviet Union.
1948   Soviet blockade of Berlin broken by Western airlift.
1949   Soviet Union backed Red China's demand for place in UN;
          Soviet Union detonated its first atomic bomb; Stalin backed
          Communist North in Korean War.
1953   Death of Stalin.

1 Introduction – Soviet Foreign Policy Before Stalin

> **KEY ISSUE** What principles underlay the foreign policy of
> revolutionary Russia after 1917?

After 1917, the Russian Communists found themselves in an odd situation. According to their own interpretation of Marxist theory, their revolution should have been soon followed by proletarian seizures of power in many other countries. This did not happen. Indeed, at one time, the very reverse seemed about to take place. During the Civil War (1918–20) there occurred a series of armed interventions in Russia, principally by France, Britain, the USA and Japan. Although these were overcome in what the Bolsheviks claimed was a major triumph over their imperialist enemies, the interventions showed the vulnerability of revolutionary Russia. Events elsewhere also indicated that any thought of an immediate Soviet-backed proletarian revolution in other countries was unrealistic. Attempted Communist revolutions in Germany and Hungary were crushed by the authorities there. A more serious reversal took place when the Soviet Red Army invaded neighbouring Poland in 1920 in the hope that the Polish workers would rise in revolution. However, the Poles, viewing the Soviet troops not as proletarian liberators but as traditional Russian aggressors, threw them out. These failures to export revolution obliged Lenin and the Bolsheviks to reconsider their role as international revolutionaries.

Lenin's response was a practical one. He considered that, since the capitalist nations were too strong and revolutionary Russia was too weak, the Bolsheviks would have to modify Soviet foreign policy. For the time being Soviet Russia would have to co-exist with other countries. This did not mean that the Bolsheviks were abandoning all thought of international revolution, only that the time was not yet ripe for a full-scale attack on capitalism. Although Lenin was a committed revolutionary, he was a realist in international affairs. He was always prepared to adjust his policies to the actual situation. In 1921 he declared, 'Our foreign policy while we are alone and while the capitalist world is strong consists in our exploiting contradictions.'

The term 'exploiting contradictions' is an instructive one. What Lenin was saying was that Soviet Russia would protect itself in a hostile world by playing on the differences that separated the capitalist nations. The conflicting self-interest of such countries as France, Britain and Germany offered an opportunity to the Soviet Union of preventing the build-up of an anti-Bolshevik alliance among the capitalist powers. Fear of western encroachment was a long-standing feature of Russian foreign policy, going back to the days of the tsars. That traditional anxiety was intensified by the bitter reaction of the governments of Europe to the 1917 Revolution and their calls for a crusade against Bolshevik Russia. In such a situation, the Soviet Union, conscious of its international isolation, became pre-occupied with securing its own defence. Compromise and survival, rather than provocation and expansion, were the guiding principles of the foreign policy that Lenin bequeathed to Stalin.

There is, therefore, an important distinction to be made between the theory and the practice of Soviet foreign policy both before and under Stalin. Judged by the propaganda it issued, Soviet Russia was pledged to the active encouragement of worldwide revolution. The Communist International organisation (Comintern) had been set up in 1919 in Moscow for this very purpose, to foment trouble and disruption in other countries. However, in practice the Bolsheviks did not regard Soviet Russia as being strong enough to sustain a genuinely revolutionary foreign policy. Their first task was to ensure the survival of the Revolution in Russia itself. This meant that whatever its aggressive poses and claims may have been, the primary purpose of the Comintern was to safeguard the existence of Soviet Russia. One of Stalin's contemporaries, Dmitri Volkogonov, later reflected: 'From a frontal attack on the citadel of imperialism, with the aim of igniting world revolution, the Bolsheviks switched to the strategy of prolonged siege'.

A major development which threw light on the character of Soviet foreign policy was the Treaty of Rapallo, signed between Germany and Soviet Russia in 1922. On the surface this was a surprising agreement between two countries opposed in character and outlook. The reason why Bolshevik Russia and reactionary Germany came together was simple necessity. They had no other choice. After 1918 they were both what Lloyd George, the British Prime Minister, called 'the pariah nations of Europe', the outcasts – Germany because of its defeat at the hands of the Allies in the Great War, and Russia because it had betrayed the Allies by making a separate peace with Germany in 1918. It would be some time before either of these two nations would be accepted on equal terms by the victorious powers of the 1914–18 War. Germany and Russia were, therefore, thrown together.

As outcasts, each had something to offer the other. The Rapallo agreement, by secretly providing German forces with training grounds in Russia, enabled Germany to flout the military restrictions imposed on her at Versailles. Russia, denied commercial contact with the rest of Europe, was able to compensate by means of the trading rights with Germany written into the Rapallo Treaty. The mutual commercial and diplomatic benefits that this gave to both countries formed the basis of a Russo-German co-operation that survived until the Nazis took power in Germany in 1933. Stalin accepted the wisdom of the pro-German policy he inherited and made no attempt to alter it. When it was finally abandoned it was not on his initiative but resulted from the virulent anti-Bolshevism of Hitler and the Nazis.

2 Anglo-Soviet Relations, 1924–29

> **KEY ISSUE** What prevented the development of co-operative relations between the USSR and Britain in the period before 1929?

Britain had been the first nation to give revolutionary Russia international recognition when, in 1921, it had signed a preliminary Anglo-Soviet trade agreement. In 1924 moves were made on both sides to expand this into a formal treaty. The joint discussions were given impetus by the coming to power in that year of the first Labour government, which despite strong criticism at home pressed on with the preparation of a draft treaty. What prevented its being ratified as a formal agreement was the scandal in Britain following the publications in *The Daily Mail*, in October, of the 'Zinoviev Letter'. This was a document marked 'very secret', written and signed by Zinoviev, the head of the Comintern, in which he called on members of the British Communist Party to infiltrate the ranks of the Labour Party and prepare the ground for armed revolution.

Historians now accept that the letter was most probably a White forgery. But at the time there were many who were eager to accept it as a genuine expression of Bolshevik intentions. The reaction to the letter indicated the fearsome image that, since 1919, the Comintern had created for itself abroad. It showed that, as long as the Comintern maintained its aggressive stance, diplomatic and commercial relations would always have to be conducted under the shadow of the political threat posed by the USSR.

The Conservative government of Stanley Baldwin, which in 1924 succeeded the short-lived minority Labour government, regarded the Soviet threat as real, and immediately withdrew recognition of the Soviet Union. In 1926, following the General Strike in Britain, the government formally accused the USSR of having improperly supported the strikers. In the following year Baldwin authorised a full-scale police raid on the London premises of a Russian trade delegation suspected of being the centre of a Soviet espionage ring. Charges and counter-charges between the two countries resulted in Britain's suspending diplomatic relations. Some improvement occurred in 1929 when Ramsay MacDonald's second Labour Government took office. Formal recognition of the USSR was restored and a new commercial agreement was discussed.

What Anglo-Soviet relations in the 1920s illustrate is that the activities of the Comintern ran counter to the diplomatic and commercial interests of the Soviet Union. It is one of the paradoxes of the period that, although the Comintern contrived to disturb other nations and so undermine Soviet trading prospects, it was never in a position seriously to advance the cause of international Communism. The result was that the Soviet Union got the worst of both worlds.

3 Stalin's Approach to International Affairs

> **KEY ISSUES** How committed was Stalin to the cause of international revolution?
> How far was Stalin responsible for the suspicion with which other nations regarded the USSR?

In view of the major influence Stalin was to have on world affairs during his quarter century as Soviet leader, it is a remarkable fact that initially he had little interest in other countries. He had seldom been out of Russia and he lacked the knowledge and experience of foreign affairs that both Lenin and Trotsky had possessed. He inherited the Comintern as the body responsible for co-ordinating schemes for international revolution but, except where it involved Soviet domestic matters, he paid scant attention to its activities. His momentous decision to adopt 'Socialism in one country' (see page 21) required that foreign policy be subordinated to the internal concerns of the Soviet Union. The Comintern continued to have a role under Stalin but it was limited to protecting the USSR. It is significant that foreign Communist parties wishing to affiliate to the Comintern had to swear absolute obedience to the line dictated by the Soviet Union. Zinoviev coined the term 'Bolshevisation' to describe this process of subjecting international Communist parties to the will of Moscow. Far from being the vanguard of international Communism, the Comintern became a branch of the Soviet foreign office. Trotsky made this very charge during the power struggle when he accused Stalin of abandoning world revolution by siding with the enemies rather than the supporters of proletarian revolution.

The dispute between Stalin and Trotsky over this was at its fiercest in regard to events in China. In 1927 Mao Zedong and the Chinese Communists (CCP) were in a desperate struggle for survival against the Nationalists (GMD), led by Chiang Kaishek. These two Chinese revolutionary parties had previously been in alliance, but Chiang had openly declared his intention of exterminating the CCP. Despite this, Stalin insisted that the alliance, which the Comintern had been instrumental in forming, must be maintained. He reasoned that Mao's Communists were too few and insignificant to be able to mount a genuine revolution: their only hope was to ally with the GMD and work for revolution on a broad front. The true proletarian revolution would have to wait. Trotsky denounced this policy as betrayal, pointing out that Stalin's interpretation of the Chinese situation was precisely equivalent to the heresy of the Russian Mensheviks in 1917 when they had argued that Russia's proletarian revolution must be preceded by a bourgeois rising based on an alliance of all the progressive parties. He condemned Stalin as the grave-digger of the Chinese revolution.

However, Stalin's victory in the Soviet power struggle effectively silenced all internal criticism of his China policy, which remained unchanged. Chiang's murderous purging of the Communists continued. Mao decided that Stalin and the Comintern were not worth dying for; he rejected their instructions and fled to safety, taking with him a distrust of Soviet motives that he was to retain for the rest of his life. Isaac Deutscher, the biographer of Stalin and Trotsky, described Stalin's attitude towards the Chinese Communists as evidence of his willingness 'to sacrifice the Chinese Revolution in what [he] believed to be the interest of the consolidation of the Soviet Union'.

1927 was not a good year for the Soviet Union. In addition to its difficulties with China and Britain, rumours of an impending invasion of Russia by the capitalist powers became widespread. In Poland, Pilsudski, the national hero who had led the successful resistance to the Red Army in 1920, had become head of government and had begun to take a strongly anti-Soviet line. If there were to be a Western attack on the USSR, the strategic danger that a hostile Poland posed for the Soviet Union would be considerable. War scares were a recurrent feature of life in Leningrad and Moscow, but the atmosphere was especially taut in 1927. Stalin and the authorities deliberately encouraged popular fears so that they could alternately cow or rally the nation. However, this is not to suggest that the war scares were wholly manufactured. The Soviet Union's often antagonistic behaviour towards the capitalist countries frequently produced strong reactions from them which tightened international tension. Today's observer can see that the mutual fears of the time were greatly exaggerated. There was never a capitalist plot for a concerted attack upon the

Soviet Union and there was never a possibility of a Soviet-organised international revolution. However, to the people of the time their apprehensions were real enough, and it was this that determined their attitude.

The USSR's difficulties with Britain and Poland did have one beneficial effect; they tended to bring the Soviet Union and Germany closer together, since both countries had good reason for fearing the rise of a powerful Poland. However, even here things did not go as well as they might. Stalin, suspicious and untrusting by nature, found it difficult to accept German good faith. In 1925 he had been disturbed by the signing of the Treaty of Locarno, a European agreement, which accepted Germany as an equal for the first time since its defeat in 1918 and opened the way to her becoming a member of the League of Nations. Although he made no effort to detach the USSR from the Rapallo Treaty on which Soviet-German relations were based, Stalin instigated a number of arrests and trials of Germans who had come to work in the Soviet Union. Historians agree that the grim record of persecution by Stalin's secret police of both Soviet nationals and foreign residents deepened the suspicion with which the USSR was regarded by other nations. It tended to make nonsense of Soviet claims that the USSR was truly a workers' state in which exploitation and suffering had been eliminated.

4 Soviet Foreign Policy in the 1930s

KEY ISSUES Why did Stalin discourage European communist parties from forming progressive alliances against fascism? How realistic was Stalin's foreign policy between 1933 and 1939?

a) 1929–33

Not everybody in the Western world took a sceptical view of the Soviet Union. There were those, usually on the political Left, who wanted to believe the best of Soviet Russia and who considered that its poor image was a deliberate distortion by the capitalist-controlled Western press. For example, many British trade unionists remained staunchly loyal to what they regarded as the Soviet experiment in workers' rule. Their influence was one of the factors prompting the second Labour government (1929–31) to renew contact with the USSR. In 1929 Ramsay MacDonald's cabinet restored formal British recognition of the Soviet Union. This was followed by the re-negotiation of a trade treaty between the two countries.

These appeared to be major diplomatic and commercial advances, but the gains were lessened by developments inside the

Soviet Union. What might be called a Left-turn is noticeable from around 1929. Stalin's victory over Bukharin (see page 25) was associated with his adoption of a much tougher approach towards other countries. This hard line was taken not so much towards the governments of those countries as towards the non-Communist parties of the Left. Orders were given that there had to be an end to all alliances between the Communist parties recognised by Moscow and the non-Communist progressive parties. Movements, such as the Labour Party in Britain and the Social Democrats in Germany, and individual socialist leaders, such as Ramsay MacDonald and Léon Blum of France, were denounced as 'social-fascists' whose only role was to delay progress towards genuine revolution. Oddly enough, real fascism, which had been in power in Italy since 1922 and was beginning to grow menacingly in its Nazi form in Germany, was largely ignored.

There is no fully satisfactory explanation for Stalin's blindness over this, but part of the answer may lie in the peculiar circumstances of the time. It was in the late 1920s and early 1930s that Stalin embarked on his massive collectivisation and industrialisation programme. This happened to coincide with the onset of the Great Depression in North America and Europe. The apparent success of Soviet economic planning contrasted with the crisis in the West, which seemed to herald the collapse of capitalism, could be interpreted as evidence of the superiority of the Soviet system. If this were indeed the case then the Soviet Union had less to fear than it had hitherto thought. It need not, therefore, bother to cultivate links with the non-Marxist socialist parties in order to broaden the basis of its protection in a hostile world. It could continue its policy of direct contact with the capitalist governments, playing upon their weaknesses and exploiting the contradictions between them.

In the long term, the USSR was to pay dearly for Stalin's failure to grasp what was happening in Germany. Before 1933, the year of Hitler's coming to power, Stalin considered that the Nazis were not strong enough to achieve their ends. He appears to have been misled by their title, National Socialist, into thinking that they might perform a useful function in preparing the ground for an eventual workers' revolution in Germany. Accordingly, it made sense for the KPD (German Communist Party) to co-operate with the Nazis. He did not appreciate that the strength and appeal of Nazism derived from its nationalism, which made it fundamentally opposed to international Communism. Such lack of insight prevented him from seeing the need to organise an alliance of German movements of the Centre and Left against Nazism. Events were to show that the KPD's obedience to the Kremlin's command not to ally with the Social Democrats had destroyed the one real chance of creating a political barrier to Nazi power in Germany.

b) Soviet Foreign Policy, 1933–39

Even after Hitler came to power in 1933, Stalin was still slow to read the signs. He tried to maintain the 11-year-old German alliance. In the end it required such developments as the violent Nazi attacks upon the KPD, open discussion among German diplomats of their country's expansion into the USSR, and the signing in 1934 of a German-Polish treaty of non-aggression, with its obvious threat to Soviet security, to convince Stalin that the spirit of Rapallo was dead. The anti-Bolshevik propaganda that the Nazis began to produce in Germany was hardly less rabid than their anti-Semitism. The USSR's greatest fear – that of isolation – returned.

For the next five years Soviet foreign policy directed itself to the task of finding allies to off-set the German danger. This has some-times been referred to as a 'turnabout' in Soviet policy, but the reality was that the USSR had no alternative. It was no longer possible to pursue a pro-German policy. Far from being a means of security, Germany was now the main threat. Tactics may have changed, but the central strategy, first introduced by Lenin, of avoiding Soviet Russia's international isolation, remained. Dominic Lieven, a modern analyst of Russian imperialism, sees an interesting parallel between Stalin's foreign policy and that followed under the last of the tsars:

> 1 In principle, Stalin, faced with the same threat, had the same options as Nicholas II. He could seek to deter and if necessary defeat this threat in alliance with the British and the French. Alternatively, he could seek to deflect German expansion westwards, hoping that the Germans, French
> 5 and British would check, weaken and exhaust each other. Meanwhile Russia could increase her relative power by devoting herself to the development of her immense resources. In 1939, after failing to come to terms with the West European allies, Stalin opted for deflection.[1]

One of the earliest opportunities for the USSR to lessen its isolation came with its admission into the League of Nations in 1934. The League provided a platform for the Soviet Union, led by its newly-appointed Foreign Commissar, Litvinov, to call for the adoption of the principle of collective security in international affairs. One of the fruits of this was an agreement in 1935 between the USSR, France and Czechoslovakia, promising 'mutual assistance' if one of the partners suffered military attack. Also in 1935, preliminary Soviet diplomatic contact was made with the USA. However, of more immediate signifi-cance was the decision, taken in that same year by the Comintern at its seventh and last Congress, to reverse its former policy of non-alignment with the Left. The Comintern now appealed for a 'popular front' in Europe of all progressive parties to combat fascism.

This was truly a turnabout in policy but it came too late. The damage had been done. European socialists, previously abused by the Soviet Union as 'social fascists', were understandably reluctant to respond to what they regarded as mere Soviet expediency in the face of German aggression. Nonetheless, Stalin pressed on with his efforts to rally international support. The new Constitution which he introduced in 1936 (see page 62) was basically a piece of propaganda aimed at convincing the outside world that the USSR was an egalitarian and democratic society.

The gains which the new approach in Soviet foreign policy achieved proved largely superficial. Collective security was impressive as a principle, but was wholly unsuccessful in practice in the 1930s. The basic weakness was that Europe's two most powerful states, France and Britain, were not prepared to risk war in order to uphold the principle. Without their participation there was no possibility of collective security becoming a reality. As the 1930s wore on and Germany became stronger, the resolve of France and Britain to act as upholders of European security appeared, in Soviet eyes, to lessen. This was certainly the inference to be drawn from Anglo-French reaction to fascist aggression in the mid-1930s. When Mussolini's Italy invaded Abyssinia in 1935 France and Britain responded not by condemning the invasion but by seeking ways to prevent it from developing into an international crisis. To this end, they were prepared to agree to a settlement with Mussolini which ceded two-thirds of Abyssinia to the Italians, leaving the native people with the remaining impoverished third. When Hitler, in direct breach of the Versailles Treaty, sent his forces to re-occupy the Rhineland in 1936, Britain and France offered formal protests but made no military moves to prevent the German takeover.

1936 was a very black year for the USSR's hopes of sheltering under collective security. In addition to the display of German aggression and Anglo-French weakness, the year also saw the creation of an international alliance aimed directly against the Soviet Union. The fascist nations, Germany, Italy and Japan, came together in November to form the Anti-Comintern Pact. The danger that this represented of a two-front attack on the Soviet Union seemed to negate all the efforts made by the Soviet Union since 1933 to establish its security. It had the effect of re-doubling Stalin's efforts to obtain reliable allies and guarantees. However, in his attempts to achieve this, Stalin was labouring under a handicap, largely of his own making. The plain fact was that Soviet Russia could not be trusted. Enough was known of the Stalinist purges in the USSR to make neutrals in other countries wary of making alliances with a nation where such treachery or such tyranny was possible.

If Stalin made it difficult for neutrals and moderates to sympathise with the defence needs of the Soviet Union, he also put barriers in the way of those on the political Left in other countries who should have been his natural supporters. His pursuit of defence agreements with the capitalist powers led to ambiguities and compromises that confused and alienated many Soviet sympathisers. This was especially so with regard to Stalin's attitude towards the Spanish Civil War (1936–39). The struggle in Spain was a complex affair, but the rest of Europe tended to see it in simple terms as a struggle between the republican Left and the fascist Right, a reflection of the basic political divide in Europe. Stalin and the Comintern, in keeping with the new Soviet policy of encouraging anti-fascist 'popular fronts', sent agents into Spain to organise an alliance of pro-Republican forces. Stalin's motives and policies were mixed. By focusing on Spain he hoped to divert foreign attention away from the current Soviet purges.

The sending of Soviet military equipment to the Republican side was not simple generosity. In payment, the Spanish Republic had to transfer the greater part of its gold reserves to the USSR. Furthermore, the 'popular front' policy meant in practice that the Soviet Union required all the Republican contingents to put themselves under Soviet direction. The Spanish Left came to resent this and to doubt whether Russia really wanted the victory of the Spanish Republic. They were correct; Stalin was anxious not to see a major victory for Marxism in Spain. The explanation of this paradox lies not in Spain, but in Europe at large. Stalin feared that, if Communism were installed in south-western Europe, this would so frighten France and Britain that they might well react by forming an anti-Soviet front with Germany and Italy, the very consequence which Soviet foreign policy was committed to avoiding.

Events in Spain had not run their full course when they were overtaken by dramatic developments in central Europe. In the autumn of 1938, France, Britain, Italy and Germany signed the Munich agreement, the climax to the Czechoslovak crisis. Hitler had demanded that the Sudetenland, an area which in 1919 had been incorporated, against the will of the majority of its inhabitants, into Czechoslovakia, be allowed to become part of Germany. He had threatened invasion if his requirements were not met. Although Hitler's demand was another breach of the Versailles settlement, neither Britain nor France was prepared to go to war over the issue. The Munich agreement granted all his major demands. This success came on top of his achievement, earlier in 1938, of the *Anschluss*, the incorporation of Austria into the Third Reich. This was in direct defiance of the Versailles settlement, which had forbidden the unification of Germany and Austria. Munich was thus a further example of Hitler's ability to get his way in Europe by exploiting French and British reluctance to contemplate armed resistance.

In the Western world the Munich settlement has customarily been seen as an act of 'appeasement', part of the Anglo-French policy of avoiding war by making timely concession to the aggressor. That was not the interpretation put upon it by Stalin. For him, Munich was a gathering of the anti-Soviet nations of Europe, intent on giving Germany a free hand to attack a diplomatically-isolated USSR. To

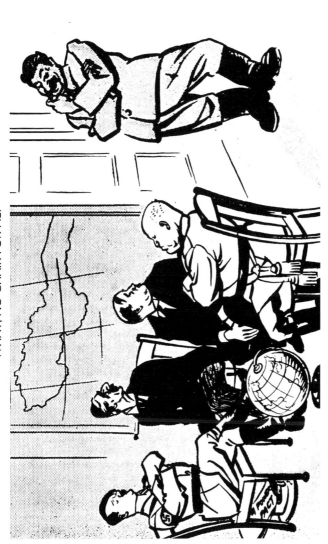

'WHAT, NO CHAIR FOR ME?'

Low's cartoon of September 1938 accurately captured Stalin's response to the Munich settlement, which formally acceded to Germany's demand for possession of the Sudenten region of Czechoslovakia. The Russian leader viewed the Munich conference, to which the USSR had pointedly not been invited despite its formal alliance of 1935 with Czechoslovakia, as a Western conspiracy. The other persons represented are Hitler, Neville Chamberlain, Daladier of France, and Mussolini.

forestall this happening, Soviet efforts to reach agreement with France and Britain were intensified. In the year following Munich, Litvinov and his successor as Foreign Minister, Molotov, delivered a series of formal alliance proposals to the French and British governments. These went unanswered. France and Britain could not bring themselves to trust Stalin. Both countries also genuinely considered that an alliance with Poland rather than the USSR offered the better protection against further German expansion.

5 The Nazi–Soviet Pact, 1939–41

KEY ISSUES Why, despite their profound ideological hatred for each other, were Nazi Germany and Soviet Russia willing to sign a non-aggression pact in 1939?
Why was Stalin unwilling to accept that the Pact had broken down in June 1941?

In August 1939 the impossible happened. Nazi Germany and Communist Russia, sworn ideological enemies, came together in a formal agreement. Molotov, the Soviet Foreign Minister, and his German counterpart, Ribbentrop, signed the Nazi–Soviet Pact, in which both countries gave a solemn pledge to maintain peaceful relations with each other.

1 The Government of the German Reich and the Government of the USSR, desirous of strengthening the cause of peace between Germany and the USSR, have reached the following agreement.
      Article I. Both High Contracting Parties obligate themselves to desist
5 from any act of violence, any aggressive action, and any attack on each other, either individually or jointly with other powers.
      Article II. Should one of the High Contracting Parties become the object of belligerent action by a third power, the other High Contracting Party shall in no manner lend its support to this third party.
10   Article III. The Governments of the two High Contracting Parties shall in the future maintain continual contact with one another for the purpose of consultation in order to exchange information on problems affecting their common interest ...
      Article V. Should disputes or conflicts arise between the High
15 Contracting Parties, both Parties shall settle these disputes exclusively through friendly exchange of opinion, or, if necessary, through the establishment of arbitration commissions.
      Article VI. The present treaty is concluded for a period of ten years ...

Secret Additional protocol
20 1 In the event of a territorial and political arrangement in the areas
belonging to the Baltic States (Finland, Estonia, Latvia, Lithuania), the
northern boundary of Lithuania shall represent the boundary of the
spheres of influence of Germany and the USSR ...
2 The question of whether the interests of both parties make desirable
25   the maintenance of an independent Polish state and how such a state
should be bounded can only be definitely determined in the course
of further developments.[2]

At the beginning of September 1939, German forces began to occupy
Poland. Four weeks later, under the terms of the Pact, Germany and
the USSR signed a formal agreement dividing Poland between them:

1 28th Sept, 1939
The Government of the German Reich and the Government of the
USSR consider it as exclusively their task, after the collapse of the
former Polish state, to re-establish peace and order in these territories.
5 To this end they have agreed upon the following:
The Government of the German Reich and the Government of the
USSR shall determine the boundary of their respective national
interests in the territory of the former Polish state ... The territory of
the Lithuanian state falls into the sphere of influence of the USSR, while
10 the province of Lublin, and parts of the province of Warsaw fall to the
influence of Germany ... Both Parties will tolerate in their territories
no Polish agitation which affects the territories of the other Party. They
will suppress in their territories all beginnings of such agitation and
inform each other concerning suitable measures.[3]

The Nazi-Soviet Pact bewildered the USSR's friends and foes alike. It
seemed to defy history and logic. An official at the British Foreign
Office dryly remarked that with the coming together of fascism and
Communism, Nazism and Marxism 'all these -isms are now -wasms'.
But there was a rationale to this remarkable change in Soviet foreign
policy. Given the real threat that Germany presented and the indif-
ference of Paris and London to his offers of a defence alliance, Stalin
felt he had been left no alternative. He had acted on the axiom 'if you
can't beat them, join them', and had attempted to nullify the danger
from Germany by the only move that international circumstances still
allowed – an agreement with Germany.

The fruits of the Pact were gathered by both countries during the next
two years. The USSR duly grabbed the eastern half of Poland. Germany
was free to conduct its war against France and Britain in the west, while
in the east the USSR added to its Polish prize by forcibly taking hold of
the Baltic states, southern Finland, and Bessarabia-Bukovina (see map
on page 97). By 1941 Soviet Russia had regained all the territories it had
lost as a result of the First World War. All this, added to the ten-year guarantee of peace with Germany, seemed to justify the praise heaped on
Stalin inside the Soviet Union for his diplomatic master-stroke.

Molotov signs the Nazi – Soviet Pact on 23 August 1939. A smiling Stalin looks on.

The extravagant claim made for the Nazi-Soviet Pact was that it had safeguarded Soviet security by a guarantee of freedom from western attack, and had thus fulfilled the chief objective for which Soviet foreign policy had been struggling since the days of Lenin. Stalin appears to have believed his own propaganda. It is one of the inexplicable things about him that he remained oblivious of Hitler's clear intention to invade and occupy Russia. An outstanding and consistent feature of Nazism from its beginnings had been its ideological conviction that Germany had a providential destiny to expand eastwards at the expense of the Slav lands, including Russia. That was the one clear strategy to be deduced from the otherwise tedious ramblings of Hitler's *Mein Kampf,* written in the 1920s and regarded as the Nazi bible. Between August 1939 and June 1941 Stalin chose to ignore all this.

It is also extraordinary that he failed to realise that the Pact, which gave Germany a free hand in the war which broke out in Western Europe in September 1939, made the German invasion of Russia likely to come sooner rather than later. The fall of France in June 1940, and the inability of Britain to do more than survive, encouraged Hitler to launch his long-intended attack upon the USSR on 22 June 1941. Operation Barbarossa, Hitler's own code-name for the invasion, was on a huge scale and the preparations for it could not be hidden. For many months before it was unleashed the USSR had known of its likelihood. When on 15 June 1941 information was passed to Stalin from Richard Sorge, a Comintern agent in Japan, which provided clear evidence that within a few days Germany would launch a massive attack on western Russia, he wrote dismissively on Sorge's message 'This is German disinformation'. On the following day Stalin received further news confirming Sorge's story, this time from Fitin, the head of Soviet Security. Fitin informed Stalin that a reliable source in the Luftwaffe had warned, 'Preparations for an armed invasion of the USSR are fully complete and the attack may be expected at any time'. Stalin's reaction was to write angrily to Fitin's boss, Merkulov, the Minister for State Security: 'You can tell your "source" in German air force headquarters to go fuck himself. He's not a "source", he's a disinformer'.

Why Stalin refused to accept the truth defies reasonable explanation. Perhaps he could not bring himself to admit that the Nazi-Soviet Pact had failed. Perhaps he genuinely believed that Hitler could still be bought off. This might explain why in 1941 he had offered more and more Soviet military and economic concessions to Germany. Yet however puzzling Stalin's reasoning, its consequences were abundantly clear. Because he was unwilling to admit the reality of the situation in June 1941 none of his underlings could take the initiative. The result was that in the first week of the Second World War on the eastern front the German forces overran a Soviet Union that was wholly without effective leadership and direction.

A remarkable feature of this was that in many areas along the invasion front the local Soviet population welcomed the invaders. Some were even willing to join the German forces. This was not from love of Germany but hatred of Stalinism. Had the German high command grasped the significance of this they might have enlisted the people of the occupied areas in a great anti-Stalin crusade. But, blinded by Nazi racial theory, they administered the areas they overran not with sympathy but with savagery and repression. The deputy leader of the German Ministry for the Occupied East, Otto Brautigam, warned of the consequences:

I In the Soviet Union we found on our arrival a population weary of Bolshevism, which waited longingly for new slogans holding out the prospect of a better future for them. It was Germany's duty to find such slogans, but they remained unuttered. The population greeted us with 5 joy as liberators and placed themselves at our disposal.
   In the prevailing limitless abuse of the Slavic humanity, recruiting methods were used which probably have their origin only in the blackest periods of the slave traffic. Our policy has forced both Bolsheviks and Russian nationalists into a common front against us. The Russian 10 fights today with exceptional bravery and self-sacrifice for nothing more or less than recognition of his human dignity.[4]

Germany was eventually to pay a terrible price for this. The Soviet people responded to German brutality by committing themselves to a desperate struggle for survival which climaxed in victory in 1945. In pushing into eastern Germany in the closing stages of the war, the Red Army subjected the civilian population to the same ferocity which the Soviet people had suffered.

6 The Grand Alliance, 1941–45

> **KEY ISSUE** Why were the relations between the Soviet Union and its wartime allies constantly under strain?

For days after the German invasion had started, Stalin sat in his dacha, refusing to speak or give instructions. Yet once he had recovered his nerve he began to provide the resolute and inspiring leadership of the USSR that was to carry it through four long years of bitter attrition to eventual victory in 1945. This was portrayed in Soviet propaganda as the triumph of Stalin's great anti-fascist crusade. However, the truth was that Stalin had not entered the war against Germany willingly. As the Nazi-Soviet Pact had shown, the object of Stalin's policy before 1941 had been to reach a compromise with Nazism, not fight against it. This had an important bearing on the nature of Stalin's relations with the USSR's principal wartime allies, Britain and the

USA. The three countries became allies not through choice but through circumstance. Before being attacked in June 1941 the Soviet Union had made no effort to assist Britain in its struggle with Germany that had begun in September 1939. Still less was the Soviet-American alliance a natural one. It came into being only after Germany, as an ally of Japan, declared war on the United States following the Japanese attack on Pearl Harbor in December 1941.

The coming together of the 'Big Three', the Soviet Union, the USA and Britain, became known as 'the Grand Alliance'. However, a more accurate description might be 'the marriage of convenience'. What bound them together was their desire to defeat the common enemy. They had little else in common. In public, frequent tributes were made to the war efforts of their glorious allies, but behind the scenes there was constant bickering between the Soviet Union and its two Western partners.

A major contention was the question of a second front. From the beginning of the alliance Stalin pleaded with the other allies to create a second military front against Germany in occupied Europe in order to take the strain off the USSR, which was bearing the brunt of the fighting. Britain's response was to promise that when sufficient forces and supplies were available a second front would be started, but also to argue that to engage in a premature invasion of Europe would be suicidal folly. Stalin retorted that neither Britain nor the USA truly understood the intensity of the war to the death on the eastern front, and that their caution was at the expense of the Russian dead. When Churchill referred to the opening of allied fronts in North Africa, Stalin taunted him by asking whether British troops were afraid to fight Germans. Churchill reacted by asking Stalin whether he had forgotten the bravery and sacrifice of the Royal and Merchant Navies in keeping the Soviet Union supplied with essential war materials from Britain and the USA.

These taunts and recriminations did not prevent personal contact being maintained between the allies, but they did indicate the lack of true understanding between them. As the war drew towards its end and the defeat of Germany became increasingly probable, the ideological differences between the USSR and the other allies, which had been largely submerged because of the need for wartime co-operation, began to resurface. There was fear in the Soviet Union that Britain and the USA would show their true capitalist colours by attempting to enlist Germany in a war against Soviet Communism. On the Western side, there was anxiety that the Soviet advance into eastern Europe and Germany heralded the start of a new period of Communist expansion.

This mutual hostility explains why, when Stalin, Churchill and Roosevelt met at the Crimean resort of Yalta in February 1945 to plan the post-war settlement, there was great tension behind the official cordiality. As a result, the agreements they reached were temporary compromises that did not settle the larger issues. On the question of the treatment of defeated Germany, it was agreed that the country would be divided into four zones, to be separately administered by the USA, the USSR, France and Britain, but there was no common understanding on a uniform system of government in the zones. Attempts to arrive at agreement on the scale of the German payment of war reparations proved equally fruitless. In the event, it was impossible to reconcile Stalin's demand that the harshest economic penalties be imposed on Germany with the Western allies' determination not to allow Russia to drain Germany dry while they were pouring in resources to prevent the country's collapse. Stalin was later to claim, in the face of Western denials, that Yalta had guaranteed the USSR 50 per cent of German reparations.

Among the most significant of the issues discussed at Yalta was the settlement of Poland. As a result of the war, the USSR had occupied Poland and had installed a pro-Soviet Provisional Government, with the promise of future democratic elections. Britain and the USA did not trust Stalin, and feared that Poland would simply become a Soviet puppet. However, the presence of the Red Army in Poland and the readiness of the Western allies to appease Stalin on some issues in order to gain concessions elsewhere led Churchill reluctantly to grant Stalin's wishes.

The same considerations generally applied to most of eastern and central Europe, which had been occupied by the Red Army in the later stages of the war. A joint 'Allied Declaration on Liberated Europe' formally committed the USSR to pursue a policy of democracy in those areas it now occupied, but Stalin's interpretation of democracy was very different from that of the other allies. The position that Stalin took was a simple one. He was determined to create a large buffer against any future German aggression, which he now equated with Western anti-Communism. He was not prepared to withdraw Soviet forces from the countries of eastern Europe until pro-Soviet governments had been installed. 'What we have, we hold', was Stalin's unyielding position. Eastern Europe would have to pay the price for Soviet security.

The differences that emerged between the powers over Poland and eastern Europe weakened such agreements as were reached at Yalta. There was deep suspicion between East and West. This was indicated by the Soviet Union's hesitation in joining the United Nations Organisation, the international body that replaced the League of Nations as a result of the Yalta agreement. It was fear of being out-numbered by the capitalist powers that led to Stalin's insistence, as a condition of the USSR's joining, on the right of the single-member veto in the proposed five-nation UN Security Council, made up of the four occupying powers of Europe plus Chiang Kaishek's China.

At Yalta, the general expectation had been that the Japanese war would continue for a number of years. It was in the light of this that Stalin did a secret deal with Roosevelt. In return for the USSR's entering the war to assist the USA, large areas of Chinese territory would be ceded to the Soviet Union after Japan had been defeated. Stalin struck a hard bargain. Later critics of Roosevelt suggested that his acceptance of Stalin's territorial demands in the Far East was an act of appeasement equivalent to Churchill's over Poland. Ironically, the USA was to have no need of Soviet help in the war against Japan. The dropping of atomic bombs on Hiroshima on 6 August 1945 and Nagasaki three days later brought a swift and dramatic end to the Pacific war. This did not prevent Stalin's keeping to the letter of the original agreement. Immediately on receiving confirmation of the Hiroshima bombing, the USSR declared war on Japan. On 14 August, when Japan formally surrendered, Stalin duly proceeded to claim the Soviet Union's territorial rewards in the Far East.

The Potsdam Conference that began in July 1945 was essentially a continuation of Yalta. The issues under discussion – Germany, reparations, eastern Europe, Japan – were the same, and produced the same antipathy between the Soviet Union and the other allies. Indeed, in the short period between the two conferences relations had deteriorated further. The Reparations commission, established at Yalta, had produced no acceptable settlement in regard to German war debts, and Soviet ruthlessness in Poland and eastern Europe suggested that Stalin was intent on imposing as rigid a system there as operated in the USSR itself. Stalin's attitude at Potsdam was even more uncompromising than it had been at Yalta. He was not prepared to concede on any of the major issues. He was strengthened in this by the fact that he was undoubtedly the dominant statesman at the Conference. Both the USA and Britain had new leaders, Truman and Attlee respectively, whereas Stalin had attended both conferences. Such continuity worked to his advantage in negotiations. Even the news, which Truman gave him during the Potsdam Conference, of the USA's successful detonation of the world's first atom bomb did not shake Stalin from his strong diplomatic position. If anything, it made him still more determined to safeguard the USSR's recently acquired gains in Europe. The concessions over Poland and eastern Europe that he had extracted from Britain and the USA at the Yalta Conference remained substantially unaltered.

In the USSR at the end of the war, Stalin gave instructions that his role in the nation's military triumph be given the highest place. Paintings, portraying him as the great war leader planning the victory of the Soviet Union, adorned all public buildings. But Stalin had been no Hitler. Although he had been brutally unforgiving of those in the military he regarded as failures, he had had the good sense to allow his generals, such as Georgi Zhukov, real freedom to direct the war. At the great victory parade held in Moscow's Red Square in 1945 it was Zhukov, mounted on a white charger, who reviewed the troops.

He made an impressive figure. Watching from the balcony above, Stalin became deeply jealous; he had originally intended to take the review himself but had changed his mind out of fear that he would not be able to control the horse.

7 The Cold War

> **KEY ISSUES** How responsible was Stalin for the onset of the Cold War after 1945?
> What was Stalin's attitude towards Germany after 1945?
> How did the USSR react to the offer of Marshall aid?
> What part did the USSR play in the Korean War?

Yalta and Potsdam were not so much international agreements as recognitions by the Western powers of the *de facto* extension of Soviet power in Europe. In that sense they were definitions of the new international divisions, known as the Cold War. This is best understood as the period, beginning in 1945 and outlasting Stalin, during which the Communist world, led by the Soviet Union, faced its great ideological enemy, the United States and its allies, in a prolonged test of nerve. Many commentators have emphasised Stalin's refusal to consider German reunification or to give up the USSR's wartime gains in eastern Europe as a major factor in creating the Cold War. It has also frequently been suggested that Stalin never fully understood the Western position.

   Yet, while this is true, it is not the whole story. The misunderstanding was two-way. There was a Soviet perspective that the West never fully appreciated. Despite the Soviet victory over Germany and the emergence of Stalin as an outstanding world statesman, the USSR post-war felt more vulnerable than at any time since the Revolution. It was largely a matter of economics. Whatever advances had been made under the FYPs, the strain of total war from 1941 to 1945 had exhausted the Russian economy; this was one reason why at Yalta Stalin had been so insistent on the issue of German reparations. His constant fear that the West intended to crush the USSR had been intensified by the war's revelation of America's awesome economic and military power. The traditional Soviet claim to possess a superior economic and cultural system would be hard to sustain in the face of post-war international realities. Since the USSR could not hope to compete on equal economic terms with the USA, Stalin calculated that the only policy available to him after 1945 was to withdraw the Soviet Union behind its new defensive barrier, provided by the wartime acquisition of eastern Europe. Germany became the new front line in this defensive system.

Map showing Soviet expansion 1939–49

a) Stalin and Germany

When the European war ended in 1945, the new political shape of the continent had already been determined. In its push westwards, the USSR had overrun a large part of eastern Europe, including the eastern third of Germany. Within that area was the capital, Berlin, lying 100 miles inside the Soviet zone. In accordance with the Yalta and Potsdam agreements, Berlin, as with greater Germany, was divided into four occupation zones. Within a short time the three areas of the city occupied by the Western Allies had amalgamated as West Berlin, which thus became a Western island in a Communist sea. This was why Stalin became so sensitive and unco-operative over the German question, always regarding Western suggestions for a settlement as the thin end of a wedge being driven into Soviet security. In 1948 he instructed the East Germans to blockade West Berlin. This was not, as the Western governments thought, merely an act of hostility; it was a desperate attempt to end the affront to Soviet security of a Western outpost 100 miles inside Soviet-controlled East Germany.

However, the USA and Britain decided to break the siege by a massive airlift of essential supplies, using the narrow air corridors; if the Soviet Union dared to interfere with the planes, it would be an act of war. In a period of 318 days the Western allies flew one and a quarter million tons of food and fuel into West Berlin. Accepting that his hand had been trumped, Stalin ordered the siege to be abandoned in May 1949.

b) Stalin, the Marshall Plan and the Truman Doctrine

Stalin's worries over Berlin had been deepened by American moves on the economic front. The abiding anxiety of the USA after 1945 was that Europe, enfeebled by war, would easily fall prey to an expansionist Soviet Union. To avoid this and so prevent the crises in the international economy that had occurred after the First World War, the United States in 1947 introduced the Marshall Aid Plan, which offered large amounts of American capital to Europe to enable it to undertake post-war economic reconstruction. The Western European nations accepted the Plan, and their recovery began. The USA's intention was expressed by General Marshall when he introduced his Plan in June 1947:

> Our policy is directed not against any country or doctrine but against hunger, poverty, desperation, and chaos. Its purpose should be the revival of a working economy in the world, so as to permit the emergence of political and social conditions in which free institutions can exist.[5]

That was not how Stalin's Soviet Union saw it. It condemned the Plan as a cover for American imperialism and linked it with the recently issued Truman Doctrine. In 1947 an over-burdened Britain had declared its intention to withdraw its forces from Greece and Turkey. Fearing that this would leave those two countries at the mercy of the USSR, as had occurred throughout the Balkans, President Truman formally promised that America would now undertake the defence of Greece and Turkey. More significant still, he announced that the USA regarded it as its duty 'to support free peoples who are resisting attempted subjugation by armed minorities or by outside pressures'. The USSR was not expressly named as an aggressor, but Truman pointedly referred to a world divided between democracy and totalitarianism. The implication could not have been clearer. Moreover, since the declaration of the Truman Doctrine preceded the announcement of the Marshall Plan by only three months, the two were indissolubly linked in Soviet eyes. Stalin's bitter reaction was angrily voiced at the UN by Vyshinsky, the Soviet representative.

1   As is now clear, the Marshall Plan constitutes in essence merely a vari-
    ant of the Truman Doctrine, adapted to the conditions of post-war
    Europe. It is becoming more and more evident that the implementation
    of the Marshall Plan will mean placing European countries under the
5   economic and political control of the United States and direct interfer-
    ence by the latter in the internal affairs of those countries. Moreover,
    this plan is an attempt to split Europe into two camps and to complete
    the formation of a bloc of several European countries hostile to the
    interests of the democratic countries of Eastern Europe and most par-
10 ticularly to the Soviet Union.
        An important feature of this Plan is the attempt to confront the
    countries of Eastern Europe with a bloc of Western European States,
    including Western Germany. The intention is to make use of Western
    Germany and German heavy industry (the Ruhr) as one of the most
15 important economic bases for American expansion in Europe, in disre-
    gard of the national interests of the countries which suffered from
    German aggression.[6]

If the announcement of the Marshall Plan had preceded rather than followed the issuing of the Truman Doctrine, there might have been a chance of the Soviet Union's accepting its good faith. This in turn might have prevented the hardening of the Cold War. The USSR's economic plight made Marshall Aid a sorely tempting offer, and Stalin for a brief period considered accepting it. But in the end, as Vyshinsky's speech illustrated, he felt that he could not risk allowing the Eastern bloc to become financially dependent upon the United States. The political dangers were too great.

It is arguable also that Cold War suspicions rendered an economic arrangement between East and West no longer feasible. Distrust of the intentions of the USA was further justified in Soviet eyes by the formation of the North Atlantic Treaty Organisation (NATO) in 1949. In the West this was represented as a defensive alliance, freely entered into by the nations of Western Europe and North America for their mutual protection. To the Soviet Union, it was a further stage in the spread of American imperialism, begun by the Truman Doctrine and the Marshall Plan. It justified the USSR's responding in kind by building a military alliance in the Eastern bloc and it proved the wisdom of Stalin's 1945 decision to develop the Soviet Union's own atomic weapon.

c) Stalin and the Korean War, 1950–53

Relations between the USA and the USSR were not eased by their contacts in the United Nations. If anything, their membership of the UN intensified their disputes. Both the General Assembly, in which all member-states were represented, and the Security Council, the permanent five-member body responsible for settling international disputes, provided platforms for propaganda and point-scoring. In the Security Council, discussion of the major international problems of the post-war world – Persia, Greece, Germany, Korea – became a constant battleground between the USSR, regularly using its veto, and the non-Communist members. Outnumbered as it was, Soviet Russia did not view the veto as a last resort but as the instrument for redressing the anti-Soviet imbalance of the Security Council.

Soviet-American rivalry in the UN was particularly pronounced over China. The Chinese Communist Party came to power there in 1949. Led by Mao Zedong it created the People's Republic of China (PRC). In gaining their victory, the Communists had driven their main enemy, Chiang Kaishek's Nationalists, from the Chinese mainland, forcing them to take refuge on the offshore island of Taiwan (Formosa). Nonetheless, the USA chose to continue recognising the defeated Nationalists as the real China and committed itself to the economic assistance and military defence of Taiwan. The USSR's response was to demand that Mao's new China replace Nationalist China at the UN and on the Security Council.

It was the China issue that lay at the base of the Cold War's first major confrontation, the war in Korea between 1950 and 1953. After Japan's defeat in 1945 Korea had been partitioned between an American-dominated south and a Soviet-dominated north. In 1950 the North Koreans crossed the dividing line of the 38th parallel with the intention of establishing Communist control over the whole country. It was once believed that the whole affair had been initiated by Mao in collusion with Stalin. However, it is now known that Mao was as much taken by surprise by the North Korean move as were the Americans. What commentators now suggest is that Stalin had colluded with Kim Il Sung, the North Korean leader, in organising the venture and that he called upon the Chinese to give support only after the fighting had started. Having been convinced by Kim that the North Koreans were capable of sustaining a major war effort against the USA, Stalin calculated that if they could bring the whole of Korea under Communist control, the benefits to the USSR would be considerable. The USA would be humiliated by being sucked into a conflict in Asia it could not win.

In contrast, the Soviet Union would gain a very powerful position in the Far East at very little cost to itself since Soviet forces would not be directly involved. What helped in this was that under the Moscow agreement of 1950 China had ceded to the USSR the control of key naval stations and rail links in Manchuria. Furthermore, the PRC governor in Manchuria had already collaborated with Stalin in a number of secret agreements which effectively left Manchuria a vassal state of the Soviet Union. In the words of one of Mao's Western biographers, Harrison Salisbury, if South Korea could now be added to this list of Soviet advantages, 'Stalin's noose around north China and Beijing would be complete'.

Stalin's reasoning gives particular significance to the USSR's decision not to attend the vital meeting of the UN Security Council in June 1950 which voted to send UN forces to Korea. Historians once believed that the USSR had miscalculated at this critical juncture by walking out of the Security Council in protest at the Western powers' refusal to recognise the PRC as the true China. It was judged that the walk-out left the other four Security Council members (the USA, Britain, France, and Nationalist China) free to vote for the sending of a UN army to Korea, knowing that the USSR could not use its veto to block the resolution. However Andre Gromyko, the Soviet foreign minister, later admitted that the Soviet Union's decision to boycott the Security Council was a deliberate move by Stalin to entice the USA into the Korean conflict.

In outcome, the war did not fulfil Stalin's hopes. The Soviet Union always denied that it was involved militarily in Korea. Technically, this was true; Soviet forces did not take part. Nonetheless, masses of Soviet weapons were used, and there were large numbers of Soviet advisers on the North Korean side throughout the three-year conflict. Yet the effort did not repay itself. The war ended in stalemate. The Panmunjom Amnesty in 1953 left Korea still divided and with no prospect of a Communist takeover in the south. A further consequence was that the USA pledged itself to the defence of Taiwan and to the continued support of Nationalist China's membership of the UN, a position that was maintained until 1972. This was hardly an advantage to the USSR. Furthermore, contrary to Stalin's original hopes, the Soviet Union's prestige had suffered. The fighting had been left to the North Koreans and the Chinese. The sacrifices they made were prodigious. Mao proudly claimed that it was Chinese not Soviet comrades who had shed their blood in the cause of international Communism.

d) Stalin's Foreign Policy in Perspective

Soviet foreign policy under Stalin was sometimes complex in its operation, but it was essentially simple in its design. He set himself the primary task of defending his country's interests in a hostile world. Having, in any practical sense, abandoned the notion of the USSR leading an international Marxist revolution, he settled for the less ambitious but equally demanding task of safeguarding national security. He never lost his deep fear of a Western invasion. No matter how powerful he and the Soviet Union became, Stalin never ceased to regard the Soviet Union as vulnerable. That is the explanation for his decision to opt for 'socialism in one country'. His domestic policies were never an end in themselves; they had to serve the needs of national defence. His often-repeated warning that unless the Soviet Union modernised 'we shall be crushed' was the simple expression of this.

The irony was that when the invasion he dreaded actually came he refused to believe it. He was at his least ready when he should have been at his most prepared. The German invasion of 1941 very nearly destroyed all that Stalin had achieved since 1929. The manner of the Soviet Union's eventual military recovery by 1945 exhausted the country economically, but at the same time made the USSR undeniably a world power and Stalin a world statesman. This, however, did not lessen his sense of vulnerability. Whatever the various causes of the Cold War, they were in part the product of Stalin's determination never to be caught out again. His refusal to contemplate the reunification of Germany or the freedom of Eastern Europe followed from this. His suspicion of the outside world in the post-war years created an atmosphere of bitterness and distrust which conditioned Western attitudes towards the USSR and shaped the Soviet Union's perception of itself. When he died in 1953 his country was locked in an implacable ideological struggle with the capitalist West, the same situation as had existed at Lenin's death in 1924.

References

1 Dominic Lieven, *Empire: The Russian Empire and Its Rivals* (John Murray, 2000), p.297.
2 In *History of the 20th Century* (Purnell, 1968), p.1659.
3 *Ibid.*, p.1660.
4 Secret Report to the Ministry of the Occupied East, 25 October 1942.
5 In Martin McCauley, *The Origins of the Cold War* (Longman, 1983), p.122.
6 *Ibid.*, pp.123–5.

Working on Chapter 5

This chapter covers Stalin's foreign policy over the whole of his period as Soviet leader. With such a large area to study, it is important that you do not get lost in detail. Your aim should be to provide yourself with enough material to understand the principles and motives behind his policy. Remember, foreign affairs cannot be studied in isolation. Internal and external policies interact. To understand Stalin's foreign policy you also need to be familiar with the domestic history of the period, as covered in Chapters 2, 3 and 4. The following central questions should help you:

How did Stalin's policy of 'Socialism in one country' influence the conduct of Soviet foreign policy?

How did Stalin respond to the rise of fascism in Europe in the 1930s?

In what sense did the Nazi-Soviet Pact of 1939 mark a turnabout in Soviet foreign policy?

Why did the co-operation between the USSR and its Western wartime allies fail to last beyond 1945?

How far were Stalin and the Soviet Union to blame for the development of the Cold War?

Summary
'Stalin and International Relations'

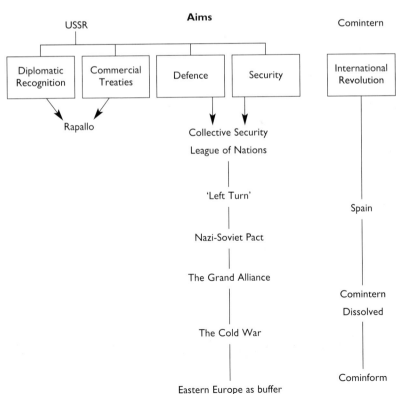

Answering structured and essay questions on Chapter 5

1. Structured questions:
a) Describe the main features of Anglo-Soviet relations between 1924 and 1929.
b) In what ways did the rise of Nazism in the 1930s affect Stalin's approach to foreign affairs?
c) Describe the agreements and understandings reached between the USSR and Germany in the period 1939–41.
d) Describe the main difficulties encountered by the USSR in its dealings with its wartime allies in the period, 1941–45.
e) In what ways did a) the nuclear issue, and b) the German question lead to a deterioration in the Soviet Union's relations with the Western powers in the period 1945–53?
2. Questions on causation:
a) Why were the Soviet Union's relations with Britain so chequered in the 1920s?
b) Why, for so long in the 1930s, did Stalin discourage Soviet co-operation with popular front movements in western Europe?
c) Explain why Stalin was deeply suspicious of the Munich agreement of 1938.
3. Questions calling for judgment:
a) How consistent was Soviet foreign policy in the period 1924–1939?
b) How acceptable do you find the argument that 'the USSR entered into the 1939 Nazi-Soviet Pact not from choice but out of necessity'?
c) How far were Soviet aims achieved at the Yalta and Potsdam Conferences of 1945?
d) Examine the validity of the assertion that 'the Cold War was largely the fault of Joseph Stalin'.

Consider question 3(a). It is not possible to comment convincingly on consistency unless you first establish whether there were any underlying objectives in Soviet foreign policy. This can best be done by drawing up a list of Stalin's aims. You should spend the first part of the answer on this aspect, stressing Stalin's basically defensive attitude. With this done, you can then turn to Soviet activities in the period 1924-39 to see how closely Stalin kept to the objectives as you have defined them. A key point to discuss is whether there was a 'turnabout' in Soviet policy in the 1930s. Whether you think there was or not is less important than that you show awareness of the issue. Your conclusion should be a re-statement of Soviet aims and an assessment of how consistently they were pursued.

Consider question 3(b). It would be an effective approach here to explain 'choice' and 'necessity' by reference to Stalin's understanding of the USSR's security needs as they had developed by 1939. 'Choice' suggests options. Did Stalin have any options left in August 1939? In answering that, you are well positioned to answer the set question.

Consider question 3(c). It would be worth your defining what

Stalin's anxieties were in regard to the position of the Soviet Union at the end of the war, and then indicate how he tried to resolve those worries by demanding a post-war territorial settlement that guaranteed Soviet security. You are then in a position to conclude whether Yalta and Potsdam provided those guarantees?

Consider question 3(d). An effective starting point would be to describe how Stalin perceived the international situation after 1945. You can then develop the answer by building on the following sub questions. Did his abiding aim of defending the Soviet Union lead him to regard his former wartime allies as potential enemies? Did he exaggerate their enmity? Were his fears realistic? How important was his manner as a negotiator and international statesman?

Source-based questions on Chapter 5

The Nazi-Soviet Pact
Read the extracts from the Pact on pages 88–9 and the September agreement on page 89 and then answer the following questions:

a) What means of mutual protection for the two Parties are laid down in the Pact? (comprehension) *(5 marks)*
b) What provisions does the Pact contain for preventing or resolving future disputes between the two Parties? (comprehension) *(5 marks)*
c) In what ways did the 'Secret Additional Protocol' prepare the ground for the division of Poland, as referred to in the September agreement? (stimulus) *(8 marks)*
d) To what extent was the September agreement a logical outcome of the secret protocol that accompanied the August Pact? (cross referencing) *(10 marks)*
e) How complete a picture of the state of Russo-German relations in 1939 is provided by these sources? (source evaluation) *(10 marks)*
f) What features of the Nazi-Soviet Pact may have suggested to Stalin that it represented a lasting settlement of Soviet-German differences? (lead out) *(12 marks)*

The Marshall Plan
Read the extract from Marshall's speech on page 98 and the extract from Vyshinsky's speech at the UN on page 99 and then answer the following questions:

a) On what grounds does Vyshinsky in his speech reject the concept of the Marshall Plan as 'the revival of a working economy in the world'? (comprehension) *(6 marks)*
b) Using your own knowledge, explain why the Soviet Union under Stalin chose to reject the offer of Marshall aid. (stimulus) *(8 marks)*
c) How far does the Marshall Plan bear out Vyshinsky's charge that it was 'merely a variant of the Truman Doctrine'? (cross referencing) *(10 marks)*

d) How valuable are these sources as examples of Soviet and American Cold War attitudes? (source evaluation) *(10 marks)*

e) How do these sources help to explain how Cold War tensions resulted in the division of Europe into two camps? (lead out) *(12 marks)*

6 The USSR Under Khrushchev, 1953–64

POINTS TO CONSIDER

The story of the Soviet Union between 1953 and 1964 is as much about the legacy of Stalin as it is about Khrushchev. This chapter examines how Khrushchev came to power after Stalin's death, his intended reform programme, and his important contribution to Cold War history as an international statesman who sought coexistence between East and West, but who also brought the world to the brink of nuclear war in 1962.

There are interesting parallels between Stalin's rise to power in the 1920s and Khrushchev's in the 1950s. Both Lenin and Stalin had failed to make any clear provision for the succession. After each one's death there was a period of collective leadership which turned into a power struggle, resulting in both instances in the victory of the least regarded or likely individual. Khrushchev rose to the leadership of the USSR in 1956 and then went on to make his mark on Soviet history. However, he was never able to wield the power Stalin had and the failure of his attempts at domestic reform and his misjudgements in foreign affairs led to his fall in 1964.

KEY DATES

1953   Death of Stalin.
1953–56 Khrushchev emerged as leader of the USSR.
1954   The 'virgin lands' policy introduced under Khrushchev.
1955   Soviet withdrawal from Austria.
                    USSR attended summit meeting at Geneva.
                    USSR signed friendship treaty with DDR (East Germany).
                    The Warsaw Pact formed.
1956   Khrushchev began the process of de-Stalinisation.
                    Khrushchev ordered Soviet forces to crush the Hungarian rising.
1957   Soviet Union launched 'sputnik', the first man-made satellite.
                    Deep Sino-Soviet hostility began to develop.
1958   Khrushchev's ultimatum to Western powers over status of DDR.
1959   Khrushchev's Seven-Year Plan started.
1959–60 Khrushchev visited a number of Western countries.
1960   American spy-plane shot down over Soviet territory.
                    Khrushchev met J.F. Kennedy, the new American President.
1961   Under Soviet orders, East Germans built the Berlin Wall.
1962   Soviet Union declined to support China in the Sino-Indian war.
                    Cuban missile crisis brought USSR-USA to brink of war.
1963   USSR signed the Nuclear Test-Ban Treaty.
                    China condemned USSR for being 'revisionist'.
1964   Khrushchev removed from power by CPSU's Central Committee.

1 Khrushchev's Rise to Power

KEY ISSUE Why was Khrushchev able to outmanoeuvre his rivals in the power struggle following Stalin's death in 1953?

Kremlin power struggles have never been easy for the outsider to disentangle, but enough evidence has come to light to provide a reasonably reliable narrative. Following Stalin's death in March 1953, the collective leadership that emerged was made up of Malenkov (Soviet Premier), Molotov (Foreign Secretary), Bulganin (Deputy Premier), and Khrushchev (Party Secretary). Their initial anxiety was that Lavrenti Beria, Stalin's chief of the MVD (the secret-police apparatus which had succeeded the dreaded Cheka) might use his organisation as a base for a power bid. The MVD certainly represented a major force in the Soviet Union, but Khrushchev was able to counter-balance it with the Red Army. The generals disliked Beria for his role in the Great Purge of the armed forces in the 1930s, and felt that Khrushchev's war record gave him a special authority; he alone of the collective leaders had actually fought in the Great Patriotic struggle. The Soviet Commander-in-Chief, Marshal Zhukov, had a particular admiration for Khrushchev. It was on the strength of this that Khrushchev was able to enlist the army's support. In June 1953 a contingent of troops surrounded Beria's apartment, blocking any possibility of the MVD's preventing his arrest. He was taken into custody, summarily tried, then shot. This was one of the few executions during the post-Stalin power struggle. The blood-lettings of the 1920s and 1930s were not to be repeated. From now on the penalty for political defeat was to be demotion or dismissal. This was one aspect of 'the thaw', the relative easing of tension and restrictions, that set in following Stalin's death.

It was due as much to Malenkov, the Premier, as anyone that 'the thaw' had begun. He had argued the need for better relations with the outside world and had suggested that attention be given to the raising of Soviet standards of living at the expense of investment in heavy industry. However, his progressive thinking brought him no political benefits. Despite being tipped by many to become the next leader, he found himself outmanoeuvred by Khrushchev. Malenkov's problem was that, despite being an able administrator, he was no match for Khrushchev in strength of personality. He lacked Khrushchev's forcefulness and persuasive ways. Another difficulty for him, similar to that which had faced the competitors to Stalin after 1924, was that Khrushchev was much better placed politically to sustain a power bid. Malenkov, as Premier, was head of government. Khrushchev, as First Secretary, was the effective head of the Party.

This enabled Khrushchev over the next two years to undermine Malenkov's position in the Soviet system. He did this not by open attack but by using his influence with Party members to criticise government ministers and their policies. He travelled widely about the countryside (something seldom done by Russian leaders, either before or after the Revolution), listening to complaints and making personal contact with a wide range of people and officials. It was a practice he continued after he came to power. He placed his own nominees in positions of authority, as Stalin had done, and began to establish a power base. By 1955 he was undoubtedly the dominant member of the collective leadership that had succeeded Stalin. It was in that year that Malenkov, publicly admitting that he was to blame for the current shortfall in grain production, resigned his premiership and gave up any thought of contending for power. He was replaced by Bulganin. For some time Bulganin and Khrushchev exercised what in appearance was a joint authority, but in reality Bulganin was very much the subordinate.

By 1956 Khrushchev felt strong enough to launch a withering attack upon Stalin's character and record. This destruction of the Stalin legend staggered Party officials and made them fear for the future because, in one obvious sense, they were all Stalinists. They had all survived to hold their current positions because they had participated in, and benefited from, Stalin's terror. Many of them found it difficult to adapt to life without Stalin. They were perplexed and frightened by the implications of Khrushchev's attack upon him. A line from a poem of the time expressed their feelings, 'We built upon granite, but now the stone crumbles, dissolves and melts at our feet.' It was around such men that an opposition to Khrushchev began to assemble. It included various disgruntled ministers and officials who had lost their positions as a direct consequence of Khrushchev's policy of decentralisation, which aimed at creating greater administrative efficiency.

Throughout Soviet history the main value of the Party to its members had been as a provider of jobs. Anyone interfering with this, as Khrushchev now was, was bound to arouse opposition. Early in 1957, while he was temporarily absent on one of his many visits abroad, the opposition made plans to remove him. Soon after his return, he had to face a concerted attack. Declaring that de-Stalinisation had gone too far and had been responsible for the recent anti-Soviet revolts in Poland and Hungary (see page 117), the Politburo voted by seven to four for his dismissal as Party Secretary. But Khrushchev proved equal to the challenge. He refused to accept the Politburo's decision unless it was backed by a vote of the full Central Committee of the Party. Using his good offices with the army, he arranged to have his own supporters specially flown in from various parts of the USSR to attend the Moscow meeting. The gamble worked. The Central Committee voted to overrule the Politburo's decision. Molotov, Kaganovich and Malenkov were then censured for having formed an 'anti-Party Group'. They duly resigned from their ministerial posts.

Having previously turned to the army as a saviour, Khrushchev now took steps to prevent its becoming a threat. Playing upon internal jealousies within the high command, he undermined the position of his long-standing supporter, Marshall Zhukov, who was accused of creating his own 'cult of the individual'. Zhukov was forced to retire, to be replaced by Marshall Malinovsky as Commander-in-Chief. It only remained to demote Bulganin, which Khrushchev did by inducing him to confess to being implicated with the 'anti-Party Group'. In March 1958 Bulganin resigned as Premier and lost his place on the Central Committee. Shortly after, Khrushchev took over that post himself. For the first time since Stalin's death, five years earlier, one man held the offices of Prime Minister in the government and First Secretary in the Party.

-Profile-

1894	born into a poor farming family in southern Russia
1909	began training as an engineer
1918	joined Bolshevik party
1918–20	served as a commissar in the Red Army
1924	entered Ukrainian politics
1931	CPSU district secretary in Moscow
1934	elected to the Central Committee
1938	First Secretary in the Ukraine
1939	joined Politburo
1942	fought at Stalingrad
1949	head of the CPSU in Moscow
1953–56	rose to prominence in the post-Stalin power struggle
1956	began process of de-Stalinisation
1956–64	became dominant figure in USSR and an international statesman

Khrushchev was born in 1894 into a poor peasant family in Kalnikova, a small town in southern Russia, close to the Ukrainian border. He received little formal education and at the age of 15 left the land to become an apprentice fitter in the mining industry. The importance of his occupation exempted him from military duty during the 1914–17 war. However, he experienced active service soon after. Having joined the Bolshevik Party in 1918, he became a Red Army commissar during the Civil War. Throughout the 1920s Khrushchev was prominent in Ukrainian affairs, serving as the Party's district secretary in a number of areas, including the capital, Kiev. In the 1930s he began to climb the Party ladder. He moved to Moscow and was appointed a district secretary there in 1931. By 1935 he had become the Party Secretary for the whole capital. Khrushchev's elevation has to be set against the background of the purges. As with all who rose within the Party or government in this period, Khrushchev was stepping into dead men's shoes. One man's imprisonment or execution was another man's promotion. The price of political survival was unswerving loyalty to Stalin, and Khrushchev was exemplary in his toadying.

For the next three years he played his part in the continuing purge of suspected anti-Stalinists in Moscow. His commitment to the task is evident in a speech he made at a Party meeting in 1936.

> 1 Just as Comrade Stalin, with his sharp Leninist eye, has accurately pointed out the path for our Party, as for the whole of the construction, so he has pointed out the corners where vermin can crawl out. We have to shoot not only this scum, but Trotsky
> 5 should also be shot. At one Moscow factory there was a young Bakaev snake [whose father had been purged] working under his own name. Yet the Party organisation didn't even know about such odious names. With a name like Bakaev, he ought to have been put under a magnifying glass. Do you call that vigilance? They've got to
> 10 learn to organise their work, how to target someone, make a rapid study of him and bring the case to a conclusion.[1]

At the end of 1938 Khrushchev went back to the Ukraine as First Party Secretary to carry out similar work there. His reward was to be made a member of the Politburo in the following year. In the war years, 1941–45, during which large parts of the Ukraine suffered German occupation, he was a political commissar in the army, involved in organising military and civilian resistance. He fought at Stalingrad and was among the Soviet forces that liberated Kiev. Immediately after the war Khrushchev returned as First Party Secretary in the Ukraine. Despite a short and obscure period in 1948 when he was suspended from office, he remained unwavering in his commitment to Stalin.

Khrushchev's reward was to be summoned to Moscow by Stalin in 1949. He was appointed Secretary to the General Committee and given particular responsibility for the planning of Soviet agriculture, an extension of the specialism he had developed as an administrator in the Ukraine. His work was not an outstanding success. One of his schemes for developing agricultural centres in the countryside, known as 'agro-towns', failed to materialise and he was criticised in *Pravda*. Such lack of success hardly suggested that he was destined for leadership. At the time of Stalin's death in 1953 Khrushchev was an industrious but not politically outstanding member of the Politburo. His breezy, talkative manner made him appear less devious and scheming than the usual Bolshevik politicians. His colleagues tended to underrate both his ambition and his ruthlessness, and yet by the late 1950s Khrushchev had come to dominate Soviet politics. As later events were to show, this did not give him absolute power. He remained answerable to the Politburo and Central Committee in a way that Stalin had never been. Nevertheless, between 1958 and his fall six years later Nikita Khrushchev was the pre-eminent Soviet figure, both as a domestic leader and as a world statesman.

2 De-Stalinisation

> **KEY ISSUES** What were Khrushchev's motives in adopting a policy of de-Stalinisation?
> How did de-Stalinisation affect the relations of the USSR with its Eastern-bloc satellites?

The process of destroying Stalin's reputation began dramatically with Khrushchev's 'secret report' to the Twentieth Congress of the CPSU in February 1956. Some signs had already appeared between 1953 and 1956 to suggest that Stalin's record might be reappraised by the new leaders of the Soviet Union. References in the press to his greatness and omniscience became less frequent and the changes in policy introduced by Malenkov were an implied criticism of Stalin's strategies. However, what was totally unexpected was the range and venom of Khrushchev's attack. In his report, which took a whole weekend to deliver, Khrushchev surveyed Stalin's career since the 1930s, exposing in detail the errors and crimes that Stalin had committed against the Party. Stalin had been guilty of 'flagrant abuses of power'. He had been personally responsible for the purges, 'those mass arrests that brought tremendous harm to our country and to the cause of socialist progress'. Khrushchev quoted a host of names of innocent Party members who had suffered at Stalin's hands. Individual cases of gross injustice were cited and examples given of the brutality and torture used to extract confessions. Khrushchev's address was frequently interrupted by outbursts of amazement and disbelief from the assembled members as he gave the details of the Stalinist terror.

Although Khrushchev's report was labelled 'secret' and was not publicly reported in the USSR until 1989, the fact was that within days the foreign Communists who had attended the Congress had leaked

A Soviet cartoon from the period of collective leadership after Stalin's death. An official is given a dose of 'criticism'.
The label on the bottle says it is a cure for 'gullibility, complacency, twaddle, conceit, bureaucratise and other ailments'.

the details to the Western press and translations appeared worldwide. These provided a vivid picture of Khrushchev's speech and the response it occasioned:

1 Of the 139 members and candidates of the Party Central Committee who were elected at the Seventeenth Congress, 98 persons, ie 70%, were shot, mostly in 1937–8. (*Indignation in the hall*) The only reason why this 70% were branded enemies of the Party and of the people was
5 that honest Communists were slandered, accusations against them were fabricated, and revolutionary legality was gravely undermined. (*Gasps from members*)

    The same fate befell not only the Central Committee members but also the majority of the delegates to the Seventeenth Party Congress.
10 Of 1966 delegates, 1108 persons were arrested on charges of counter-revolutionary crimes. This very fact shows how absurd, wild and contrary to common sense were the charges of counter-revolutionary crimes made against a majority of the participants in the Congress. (*Indignation in the hall*)
15 We should recall that the Seventeenth Party Congress is historically known as the Congress of the Victors. Delegates to the Congress were active participants in the building of our socialist state; many of them fought and suffered for Party interests during the revolutionary years and at the Civil War fronts. How then can we believe that such people
20 could prove to be 'two-faced' and join the camp of the enemies of socialism during the era of the liquidation of the Zinovievites, Trotskyites and Rightists and after the great accomplishments of socialist construction? (*Prolonged applause from members*)

    An example of vile provocation, of odious falsification, and of crimi-
25 nal violation of revolutionary legality is the case of the former candidate member of the Central Committee, Comrade Eikhe, who had been a Party member since 1905. (*Commotion in the hall*) Eikhe was arrested 29 April 1938, on the basis of slanderous materials. He was forced under torture to sign a confession in which he and several other eminent
30 Party workers were accused of anti-Soviet activity. On 4 February Comrade Eikhe was shot. (*Indignation in the hall*) It has been definitely established now that Eikhe's case was fabricated. He has been posthumously rehabilitated. (*Applause from members*)[2]

Khrushchev did not limit himself to the purges in his denunciation of Stalin. He attacked him for his failures in foreign policy, particularly with regard to the Eastern-bloc countries. He also ridiculed the idea of Stalin as a war hero, pointing out his incompetence as an organiser and strategist; one of Khrushchev's jibes was that Stalin had used a globe rather than a detailed map to plan the defence of the Soviet Union. The special term that Khrushchev used to describe the Stalinism that he was condemning was 'the cult of personality'. He explained that he meant by this that all the mistakes perpetrated in the Soviet Union since the 1930s had been a consequence of Stalin's lust for personal power, his 'mania for greatness'.

It is significant that although Khrushchev read out a long list of Stalin's victims, who were now to be officially pardoned, it did not go back before 1934 and did not include such names as Trotsky or Bukharin. Khrushchev's list was a selective one. His purpose was to blacken Stalin's name, not to criticise the Communist Party. It was important that the illegality and terror he was exposing should be seen as the crimes of one individual. In theory and in practice the Party was the essential source of power in the Soviet system, and Khrushchev was anxious not to challenge the justification for his own authority.

By any measure Khrushchev's 'secret' speech was a remarkable event in Soviet and Communist history. For a quarter of a century before 1953 Stalin had exercised astonishing power. Having destroyed his opponents, he had assumed an unchallengeable leadership. Revered as Lenin's heir, Stalin had come to personify Communism itself. To attack such a legend so soon after Stalin's death created a real danger of disruption within the Soviet Union and in the ranks of international Communism.

Why, then, did Khrushchev do it? De-Stalinisation had three basic aims: to justify the introduction of more progressive economic measures within the USSR, to make co-existence with the West easier, and to absolve Khrushchev and the other Soviet leaders from their complicity in Stalin's errors. This last aim was of particular importance. Criticism of Stalin personally was the only way to explain the otherwise inexplicable failures of the Soviet system during the post-Lenin era. Khrushchev was taking a risk in undermining Stalin's reputation. He knew that he was laying himself open to the charge of having been an accessory to the offences that he was now condemning. After all, he had helped carry out the purges in Moscow and the Ukraine. But Khrushchev calculated that, since all the Soviet leaders had climbed to their present positions by carrying out Stalin's orders, none of them had a clean record. Their shared guilt would prevent any serious challenge being offered to his denunciation of Stalin.

At the time, the peoples of the Soviet satellites and many observers in the West interpreted these developments as signs that the USSR was moving towards tolerance and freedom. They were mistaken. De-Stalinisation was never intended to be a genuine liberalising of Soviet society. It is true that large numbers of political prisoners were released from the Gulag, the labour camps which had proliferated under Stalin. There was also some lifting of State censorship. However, these were gestures rather than a wholesale abandonment of Soviet totalitarianism. At no time did Khrushchev denounce Stalin for having terrorised the Soviet people. The charge against him was always expressed in terms of crimes against the Party. By concentrating his attack on Stalin's 'cult of personality' Khrushchev was placing

the responsibility for the errors of the past on one man. The reputation and authority of the Party were thereby undiminished. This left
the new leaders of the Party free to introduce changes of policy and
strategy. Khrushchev considered that without de-Stalinisation it would
be impossible to achieve the necessary reform of the Soviet Union.

a) De-Stalinisation and the Soviet Satellites

Yugoslavia had been the one eastern-European country to have successfully resisted Soviet domination in the post-war period. It
remained Communist but independent of the USSR. In launching his
programme of de-Stalinisation at the Twentieth Party Congress in
1956, Khrushchev made great play of Stalin's mishandling of Tito and
the Yugoslav Communists. Khrushchev contended that, had Stalin
shown any real understanding of Tito and the national cause he represented, Yugoslavia would never have broken away from the Soviet
bloc:

1 I recall the first days when the conflict between the Soviet Union and
   Yugoslavia began artificially to be blown up. Once, when I came from
   Kiev to Moscow, I was invited to visit Stalin, who, pointing to the copy
   of a letter lately sent to Tito, asked me 'Have you read this?'
5   Not waiting for my reply, he answered 'I will shake my little finger
   and there will be no more Tito. He will fall'.
      We have paid dearly for this 'shaking of the little finger'. This state-
   ment reflected Stalin's mania for greatness, but he acted just that way.
   'I will shake my little finger and there will be no more Tito. I will shake
10 my little finger and many others will disappear.'
      But this did not happen to Tito. No matter how much or how little
   Stalin shook not only his finger but everything else that he could shake,
   Tito did not fall. Why? The reason was that in this case of disagreement
   with the Yugoslav comrades Tito had behind him a state and a people
15 who had gone through a severe school of fighting for liberty and independence, a people which gave support to its leaders.
      You see to what Stalin's mania for greatness led? He had completely
   lost consciousness of reality; he demonstrated his suspicion and haugh-
   tiness not only in relation to individuals in the USSR, but in relation to
20 whole parties and nations.
      We have carefully examined the case of Yugoslavia and have found a
   proper solution which is approved by the classes of all the people's
   democracies and by all progressive humanity. The liquidation of the
   abnormal relationship with Yugoslavia is done in the interest of the
25 whole camp of socialism, in the interest of strengthening peace in the
   whole world.[3]

It is unclear how seriously Khrushchev intended his reference to
improved Soviet relations with the socialist camp to be taken. His
main purpose appears to have been to reveal Stalin's foreign policy

failures. He was not calling for a revision of Eastern-bloc Communism. Nonetheless, that was how many of the Soviet satellites saw it. They read Khrushchev's attack on Stalin over Yugoslavia as an invitation to seek greater national independence for themselves. Khrushchev visited Tito in 1955 and 1956. This bestowal of Soviet favour strengthened the idea that, with Stalin gone, the Kremlin had accepted Yugoslavia's right to develop its own brand of Communism. If it was permissible for Yugoslavia, then why not for the other satellites? Throughout the Eastern bloc there were stirrings of independence. The response was particularly marked in Poland and Hungary. In the former, strong demands were made for the Polish people to be left free to develop their own form of socialism. Facing mounting pressure, Khrushchev and the Kremlin leaders compromised for a time by allowing the popular Polish patriot Gomulka, who had been outlawed in Stalin's day, to return to political prominence. However, Gomulka had to promise to discourage 'revisionism' in Poland and to renew the commitment of his country to the Warsaw Pact, the agreement signed in 1955 under direction from Moscow in which all the iron curtain countries committed themselves to the collective defence of Soviet Europe against 'Western imperialism'. The Pact was regarded as the touchstone of satellite loyalty to the USSR.

How determined the USSR under Khrushchev was to maintain its grip was clearly revealed in its reaction to events in Hungary in 1956. In its early stages the Hungarian 'thaw' seemed to be acceptable to Moscow. Imre Nagy who, like Gomulka, had been denied public office during the Stalin years, was allowed to return as the new Hungarian leader. Appearances were deceptive. When the Nagy government began to tolerate, if not encourage, popular anti-Soviet demonstrations, Khrushchev decided things had gone too far. Angered by Western attempts to raise the Hungarian independence issue in the UN, by the declared intention of the Budapest government to open politics to non-Communists and, most disturbing of all, by Nagy's plan to withdraw Hungary from the Warsaw Pact, the Kremlin ordered the long-threatened invasion. Russian tanks entered Budapest and the Hungarian 'liberal experiment' was crushed.

Khrushchev's heavy hand in Hungary was clear proof that de-Stalinisation had never been intended as a softening of the USSR's fundamental attitude. When the Soviet Union felt its own security threatened or its control of the Eastern bloc challenged, it was prepared to use force against its satellites. De-Stalinisation was a false dawn for those who thought it signified genuine independence for Eastern Europe. Khrushchev was as determined as his predecessor had been to assert the USSR's right to dictate to the rest of the socialist world. This resulted in post-Stalinist Russia strengthening, not weakening, its hold over its satellites.

3 Khrushchev and the Soviet Economy

> **KEY ISSUE** What problems faced Khrushchev in his efforts to reform the Soviet economy?

a) Agriculture

It was not long after Stalin's death that the Soviet leaders began to admit that the collectivisation of agriculture had not solved the problem of food production and supply. In 1953 Khrushchev informed the Central Committee that grain stocks under Stalin had been lower than under the last tsar. Major changes were needed, he argued. Proud of his peasant origins, Khrushchev claimed a special knowledge of agriculture. He made a point of going to meet the peasants in their own localities to urge them to adopt more efficient techniques. His broad strategy was to encourage local decision-making. As an incentive to production, the State authorities under Khrushchev's prompting began to pay higher prices to the peasants for their grain; taxes on farming profits were reduced and experts were sent from Moscow to work and advise at local level. The machine tractor stations (MTS) built in Stalin's time were sold to the farmers. The relative success of the incentive scheme can be gauged from the statistic that between 1952 and 1958 farm-workers' incomes more than doubled. Although farm wages were still much lower than those of industrial workers, prospects of real economic advancement were greater than at any time since the NEP.

The initiative most closely associated with Khrushchev at this time was the 'virgin lands' policy, introduced in 1954. This developed into a massive project for exploiting the previously unused areas of the Soviet Union for crop production. The regions earmarked for particular attention were Kazakhstan and southern Siberia. Over a quarter of a million volunteers, mainly drawn from Komsomol (the Young Communist League), were enlisted to work in these regions. Considerable financial and material investment was put into the scheme, most spectacularly in the provision of 120,000 motorised tractors. Six million acres were freshly ploughed in the virgin lands in the first year of the scheme.

There was no doubting the enthusiasm which the policy aroused. But enthusiasm was not enough. The goodwill of the volunteers could not compensate for poor management and short-sighted planning. Too little allowance was made for local conditions. Crops were often sown in unsuitable soil and the effects of climate tended to be ignored. The necessary fertilisers were seldom available in sufficient quantity. In the drive to convert to foodstuffs, successful crops such as cotton were replaced by crops such as maize which simply refused to grow. This occurred notably in Kazakhstan where the 'maize mania' often led to whole areas abandoning their traditional planting for the lure of a crop whose yield then proved so poor that it was not worth harvesting. The failure to provide adequate drying and storage facilities frequently meant that such crops as were gathered rotted before they could be distributed. Khrushchev had not been well served by the officials responsible for turning his schemes into reality.

Although there was an increase in Soviet grain production in the 1950s, this was because of greater output in the traditional areas of cultivation rather than in the virgin lands. Official talk of record Soviet harvests, as in 1962, could not disguise the fact that in few areas had production met the set targets. 1963 proved to be a disastrous year. A combination of poor weather and exhausted, under-fertilised, soil led to a drop of nearly one third in the expected grain output. This created an acute shortage in animal fodder, which in turn led to slaughter and a sharp decrease in livestock. To avoid what threatened to become a famine, large quantities of North American and Australian grain had to be purchased. What had begun as a grand design to enable the USSR to overtake the Western countries in agricultural production was in the end sustained only by buying supplies from those countries.

b) Industry

There was nothing original about the industrial policies adopted by Khrushchev. As in foreign affairs, he continued the strategies begun by Malenkov before he had been eased out of office. The difference was that Khrushchev applied the policies with a remarkable vigour. He had what in the West would be classed as a feel for public relations. Khrushchev wanted to alter the direction of the Soviet economy by lessening Soviet dependence on heavy industry and giving greater prominence to light engineering and chemicals. He emphasised the need for sustained effort, but whereas Stalin had used coercion Khrushchev offered incentives. Stalin's deliberate neglect of consumer goods was replaced by the promise of material rewards. In a radio broadcast Khrushchev excited the interest of many Soviet women, and no doubt some of the men, by suggesting that if they continued to work hard they would soon be able to buy nylon underwear.

Contemptuous of the huge bureaucracy that had grown up under Stalin, Khrushchev was eager to see administration streamlined and decentralised. His hoped that by transferring decision-making from the centre to the localities planning would prove more realistic and progressive. However, the attempt to reduce central authority offended the entrenched bureaucrats. Those many Party members and government officials who owed their positions to Stalin's preferment did not look kindly on reforms that threatened their privileges.

Stalin had structured the Soviet economy around the Five-Year

Plans. At his death in 1953, the Fifth Plan had run half its course. Its emphasis, as with the preceding ones, had been on heavy industry. When Khrushchev, continuing where Malenkov had left off, sought to redirect industry towards consumer production he had to break down the resistance of planners who had been trained to believe that consumer goods were of only marginal importance. They still measured economic success by counting iron and steel output. This was a legacy of Stalin's concept of a siege or war economy. It is true that even after Stalin the USSR remained heavily committed to military development in both the nuclear and conventional fields, but it was Khrushchev's genuine belief that if this could be lessened the economic freedom it would give would provide the Soviet Union with the potential to catch up with the West. The USSR's lead in space technology, a by-product of its missile programme, was a remarkable but isolated achievement. It was not matched in any other aspect of its economy.

A Sixth FYP was introduced in 1955, only to be scrapped as being too optimistic and replaced by a Seven-Year Plan in 1959. Under Khrushchev's instructions this Plan had been drawn up with the aim of promoting consumer goods, light industry, chemicals and plastics. In addition, stress was placed upon the need for regional development. Less spectacularly than in agriculture, but no less significantly, Khrushchev was attempting to reverse a major feature of Stalin's policy. It was a recognition that the USSR could not develop as a modern state unless it brought a much greater degree of balance into its economy. An idea of how far Khrushchev's industrial policies succeeded during the period of his leadership can be gained from the performance figures below, comparing the targets in the Seven-Year Plan with the actual performance in 1965:

	Plan	Actual
Gross National Income (calculated from a unit of 100 in 1958)	162–165	158
Output		
Industrial goods (unit of 100 in 1958)	185–188	196
Consumer goods (unit of 100 in 1958)	162–165	160
Steel (million tons)	86–91	91
Oil (million tons)	230–240	242
Mineral Fertilisers (million tons)	35	32
Grain (million tons)	164–180	121
Meat (million tons)	6.1	5.25
Workers employed (millions)	66.5	76.9
Total of Available Housing (million square metres)	650–660	72.9

Set against the general success of the Seven-Year Plan, the obvious and serious failures were in under-production of grain and meat, and in the inability to deal with the perennial Soviet problem of shortage of accommodation.

4 Co-Existence with the West

> **KEY ISSUE** How far did Khrushchev's pursuit of co-existence mark a departure from traditional Soviet policy towards the West?

The policy of co-existence, as pursued by Khrushchev, was the practical recognition of the right of individual nations to operate the political and social systems of their choice. The acceptance of this right marked a major change of direction in Soviet attitudes to the outside world. The revolutionaries of 1917 had seen themselves as crusaders, intent on fighting the international class war foretold by Marx. The realities of world politics had obliged Lenin and Stalin to suspend the pursuit of this objective, but the commitment to international revolution had never been formally abandoned. Khrushchev, in his secret speech to the Twentieth Party Congress in 1956, took the highly significant step of declaring that a violent conflict between the Communist and capitalist world was not inevitable in the way that Lenin had described. This declaration helped to prepare the way for the moves towards co-existence that characterise Soviet foreign policy under Khrushchev in the decade after 1956.

The path towards better relations with the West had already been smoothed by a number of developments in the period after Stalin's death. The Korean War, which had soured international relations, ended in 1953. In the following year the USSR joined with the USA and Britain at Geneva in helping to negotiate the withdrawal of French forces from Indo-China. In 1955 the Soviet Union signed a peace treaty with Austria and recalled the army of occupation, stationed there since 1945. The easier atmosphere, referred to as 'the spirit of Geneva', that all this created led the USSR to attend a summit conference in Geneva in the summer of 1955. Khrushchev and Bulganin met President Eisenhower and the French and British Prime Ministers. Although no major agreements were reached, the greater cordiality produced by personal meetings at top level encouraged Khrushchev to believe that the Soviet Union stood to gain by following a policy of co-existence with, rather than hostility towards, the West.

Accompanied usually by Bulganin, he began a series of visits to countries outside the Eastern bloc, something that would have been unthinkable in Stalin's time. India, China, Yugoslavia, Britain and the USA were among the countries visited. On the whole these travels were a propaganda success. He was able to boast of Soviet achievements in space, calling particular attention to the launching of the 'Sputnik' satellite in 1957. He defended the Soviet system with great passion and considerable wit, showing the West that there was a human face to Soviet leadership. He made a remarkable impact in the United States. In Hollywood he watched the filming of one of the dance sequences from 'Can Can', which by Soviet standards was a trifle saucy. When asked what he thought of it, Khrushchev said it was indecent, decadent and bourgeois – and could he see it again?

It was while in the USA that Khrushchev first declared that the development of nuclear weapons in both East and West had made war unthinkable; the differences between the Communist and capitalist worlds would have to be settled by other means. His meetings with Eisenhower in 1959 at Camp David were considered so constructive that they gave rise to the term 'the spirit of Camp David' as an expression of the improved Soviet-American understanding. However, it soon became clear how fragile this understanding was when set against the underlying reality of the Cold War. In 1960 a Paris summit conference broke up in acrimony when Khrushchev announced that the USSR had tracked and shot down an American U2 reconnaissance-plane spying over Soviet territory. Khrushchev made an issue of Eisenhower's refusal to apologise and stormed dramatically out of the conference. A meeting with the new American President, J.F. Kennedy, in Vienna in 1961 proved cordial but it did not repair the earlier damage. Indeed, despite their apparent mutual respect, Khrushchev and Kennedy were shortly to be at loggerheads over the most dangerous East-West confrontation of the Cold War, the Cuban missile crisis of 1962.

As a way of lessening international tension, co-existence had an obvious appeal, but it proved hard to sustain in the face of the recurrent crises over such unresolved Cold War issues as Germany and the arms race. Nonetheless, it was in regard to the arms race that Khrushchev gained the greatest success in his policy of co-existence, the signing by the super-powers of a Nuclear-Test Ban Treaty in October 1963. The agreement between the USA and the USSR to abandon nuclear detonations in the atmosphere was the first major accord on arms limitation in the history of the Cold War.

5 Khrushchev and Germany

KEY ISSUE Why did the Soviet Union regard the German question as 'a fish bone in the gullet'?

Khrushchev inherited a chronic problem in the shape of the German question, which preoccupied him for the whole of his leadership. By the mid 1950s the economic and political divisions between Western and Eastern Germany and between West and East Berlin had become an enduring reality. Sustained by Marshall Aid from the late 1940s on, West Germany and West Berlin began to make a remarkable economic recovery. This contrasted sharply with East Germany and East Berlin, where a lack of resources and investment resulted in severe poverty. This disparity became a scandal and an embarrassment to the East German authorities and the Soviet Union. Nor was it simply a matter of economics: the political freedom and open life-style of the West Berliners proved a powerful temptation to East Germans, which no amount of Soviet propaganda could dispel. In the eight years after 1949 over two million refugees fled from East Germany to the West, by way of West Berlin. Many of these were professional and skilled workers whom the DDR (East Germany) could ill afford to lose.

This was the chief problem that Khrushchev confronted. He spoke of his intention to 'block up the drain'. His first moves were to try to force the Western powers to recognise the existence of a separate state of East Germany, something which they had consistently refused to do. In 1955, a USSR-DDR treaty was drawn up, granting East Germany full freedom in the conduct of its foreign affairs. However, in an official Note to the USA Khrushchev announced that the USSR would continue to decide any questions relating to rights of movement between West Berlin and West Germany:

> As for control over the movement between the German Federal Republic [West Germany] and West Berlin of military personnel and freight, of garrisons of the USA, Great Britain and France quartered in West Berlin, in negotiations between the Governments of the USSR
> 5 and the German Democratic Republic, it was stipulated that this control would henceforth be carried out by the command of the Soviet military forces in Germany temporarily until the achievement of a suitable agreement.[4]

Khrushchev's Note was part-threat, part-offer, to the West. By retaining responsibility for all questions of access to Berlin the Soviet Union was delaying the moment when the West would have to deal directly with East Germany. If the West ignored his offer and refused to recognise the legitimacy of the DDR, then the USSR would hand over to East Germany control of the access routes. This would force the West to recognise the DDR, since there would be no alternative to direct relations with it once the USSR withdrew. It would also destroy the fiction with which the West still persisted, that East Germany was merely the Soviet zone of occupied Germany.

In the event, the USA called his bluff by refusing to change its stance on Germany. By 1958 the DDR had still not gained formal Western recognition as a sovereign state. To press the issue, Khrushchev informed the West that the Soviet Union intended to grant the DDR complete management of its own affairs. He then delivered an ultimatum. In strident language he accused the West of using West Berlin 'as a springboard for espionage and anti-Soviet acts'. He warned that, if within six months the West had not responded positively, the USSR would sign a separate peace treaty with the DDR. This would directly threaten the independence of West Berlin since, as a sovereign state, the DDR would have the right to claim the whole of its capital, Berlin:

1 Berlin is a smouldering fuse that has been connected to a powder keg. Incidents arising here may, in an atmosphere of heated passions, suspicions and mutual apprehensions, cause a conflagration which will be difficult to extinguish.

5 The Soviet Government proposes to make no change in the present procedure for military traffic of the USA, Great Britain and France from West Berlin to the Federal Republic of Germany for half a year. If the above period is not utilised to reach an adequate agreement, the Soviet Union will then carry out the planned measures through an agreement 10 with the DDR.[5]

The ultimatum created an international crisis, but it is unlikely that Khrushchev was doing more than testing how committed the West was to the defence of Berlin. The Western powers pointedly delayed their formal reply to his Note, but let it be known that they regarded the six-month ultimatum as outrageous. When the USA did reply it was to reassert the absolute right of continued free access to West Berlin. Faced with this, Khrushchev withdrew the ultimatum and at a summit meeting in March 1959 admitted the rights of the three occupying powers in West Berlin. In a series of meetings, first with Eisenhower and then with J.F. Kennedy, Khrushchev modified his demands but continued to insist that the Berlin question, 'that fishbone in the gullet' as he called it, must be resolved.

Having tried the gentler approach, Khrushchev then returned to the attack. In June 1961 he met Kennedy again. This time he repeated his warning that the Western powers must be prepared to leave Berlin within six months. The effect of this threat was to increase the flight of refugees from East to West Berlin; a thousand a day became the average figure in the summer of 1961. Unable to staunch the haemorrhage, the East German leader, Walter Ulbricht, ordered the construction of the Berlin Wall. This grim construction of drab concrete, which split the city in half, became the physical symbol of the ideological East-West divide.

Initially, there were fears that the Wall would lead to open conflict. However, in an odd way it created greater international understanding. It clarified the diplomatic differences that had led to its construction and, by stopping the loss of essential manpower, it saved East Germany from economic collapse. This helped to restore stability and so lessened the likelihood of desperate measures being taken by the East Germans, which the Soviet Union would then have had to support and the West would have had to resist.

Khrushchev's last initiative on the German issue was an attempt to win by persuasion what he had not gained by threat. In 1963 he made formal contact with the West German government and let it be known that he was prepared to solve the Berlin issue by by-passing the East Germans and negotiating directly with Bonn. This was a drastic reversal of Soviet policy and provoked an understandably bitter response from Ulbricht and the East Germans. The change also puzzled many in the Soviet Union. Khrushchev had apparently become convinced that there was no future in enforcing a German settlement on the West. That had been tried and had failed. Approaching the West German government directly was a striking piece of diplomacy that might well give the USSR an advantage in future negotiations. There were also rumours that Khrushchev found Ulbricht and the East German government a wearisome bunch, whom he preferred to ignore if he could. Yet whatever Khrushchev's motives may have been, they soon became academic. Before anything could come of his new German policy, he had been removed from office in the Soviet Union.

With hindsight, it can be seen that Khrushchev's policy towards Germany was shaped as much by the pressures upon him in the Soviet Union as by the intrinsic merits of the question. Khrushchev was conscious that his style of leadership needed positive successes in order to justify itself. He was constantly under scrutiny. Had he been able to resolve the German and Berlin issues this would have been an outstanding achievement, and would have enhanced his position in the USSR. At most stages, however, he was thwarted by the strength of the United States' commitment to West Germany. In addition, the persistent economic weakness of East Germany undermined Khrushchev's diplomatic bargaining position. He was never able to realise his main aim of obtaining Western acceptance of separate German peace treaties. Behind Khrushchev's threat and bluster lay his sure knowledge that a genuine settlement of the German problem could not be gained by unilateral Soviet action. It would require a binding agreement between the USA and the USSR. The construction of the Berlin Wall in 1961 marked the failure of Khrushchev's German policy. He and the USSR had suffered a serious international reverse. His subsequent behaviour in 1962 in regard to Cuba may well represent his attempt to recover the prestige he had lost.

6 The Cuban Missile Crisis, 1962

KEY ISSUES How far was Khrushchev responsible for the onset of the crisis?
Did the Soviet Union derive any positive results from its involvement in the crisis?

When Fidel Castro, the revolutionary leader of Cuba since 1959, openly declared himself a Communist and began to take steps to end the USA's economic domination of the island, Khrushchev saw the possibility of a major Cold-War coup. He moved quickly, arranging for the Soviet Union to buy up Cuba's sugar crop and offering a package of economic assistance. The attraction of Cuba for the Soviet Union was obvious. It provided an opportunity for the USSR to establish a foothold in the western hemisphere. The Soviet Union hoped, and the USA feared, that the creation of a Russian-backed Marxist state in Cuba would be the prelude to the rapid spread of Soviet-style Communism throughout central and South America.

Aware of United States' alarm over these developments, Khrushchev warned that the USSR would be prepared to act if the USA used force against Cuba. The Soviet Union increased its investment and involvement in Cuba, culminating in 'Operation Anadyr', the installation on the island of Soviet nuclear missiles, capable of reaching almost every state in the USA. Malinovsky, the Soviet Defence Minister, reported to Khrushchev that he was carrying out his instructions 'to turn the island into an impregnable fortress. Missile forces must be ready on a signal from Moscow to launch nuclear missile strikes on important targets in the United States.' Throughout the Cuban affair Khrushchev was involved in every aspect of the planning. Dmitri Volkogonov, the Soviet historian, offers a fascinating explanation of why Khrushchev was so personally committed:

1 Khrushchev was elated. He had not felt like this since his days as a member of the Military Council at Stalingrad and Kursk, during the war. Then, however, he had been carrying out Stalin's will, whereas now it was he who was generating the ideas and exercising the decisive will to
5 bring off this vast enterprise, which required huge resources and a great concentration of forces.[6]

In private conversation Khrushchev spoke of 'putting one of our hedgehogs down the Americans' trousers'. However, his publicly-stated justification for Soviet actions was that the nuclear devices were there to defend Cuba against possible American intervention. But, since this claim followed a previous denial that the USSR had installed any missiles at all, the argument was unconvincing. Kennedy announced a naval blockade of Cuba until the missiles were removed, and let it be known that if any attempt were made to use them against the USA he would order a retaliation in kind. When Khrushchev likened the proximity of Russian weapons in Cuba to that of American missiles in Turkey, the USSR's neighbour, Kennedy replied that the American rocket-bases were there to defend Europe, whereas the only conceivable purpose of the Soviet missiles in Cuba was to threaten the USA with direct nuclear attack. Kennedy backed his ultimatum by placing the US armed forces on nuclear war alert.

Faced by such uncompromising determination, Khrushchev chose not to risk a full-scale nuclear confrontation. He gave the order for the Soviet ships which were approaching the exclusion zone to put about and not to challenge the American naval blockade. With the tension broken, direct contacts by letter and phone were made between Kennedy and Khrushchev. Their exchanges produced a compromise; the Soviet leader agreed to order the withdrawal of Soviet missiles from Cuba and the American President gave a commitment to reduce the USA's bases in Turkey. This latter agreement was a significant gain for the USSR, but at the time it was overshadowed by what observers in the Soviet Union regarded as a major diplomatic victory for the Americans. It had been the USSR which had backed off. The USA had reasserted its paramount influence in the western hemisphere. This apparent defeat damaged the USSR's international standing and led to serious criticism of Khrushchev within the Soviet Union. At the time of his dismissal in 1964, the report of the CPSU's Central Committee included this passage:

> 1 Comrade Khrushchev declared that if the USA touched Cuba we would launch a strike against it. He insisted that our missiles be sent to Cuba. This provoked the most serious crisis, bringing the world to the brink of nuclear war; the organizer of this most dangerous venture himself
> 5 was greatly alarmed. Having no other way out, we were forced to accept all the demands and conditions dictated by the USA.[7]

7 Khrushchev and China

> **KEY ISSUES** Why did the two Communist super-powers fall out with each other?
> How much of the Sino-Soviet rivalry was due to the personalities of Khrushchev and Mao Zedong?

The coming to power of the Chinese Communist Party (CCP) under Mao Zedong in China in 1949 had been greatly welcomed in Moscow. It was logical for the Soviet Union to think that it now had a major Marxist ally in its Cold-War struggle with the West. Indeed, that is precisely what the West feared, the formation of a huge Soviet-dominated Marxist power-bloc that stretched eastwards from Europe to the Pacific. But appearances were deceptive. There was little real harmony between Moscow and Peking. Relations between the USSR and Communist China had never been easy. Stalin's Russia, pre-occupied with its own internal problems, had failed to grasp the significance of developments in Mao Zedong's China (see page 81).

The fundamental issue in Sino-Soviet relations was the competition to decide which power was the real leader of the Communist world. Was it the USSR, product and guardian of the great 1917 revolution, or the People's Republic of China with its fresh revolutionary ideas and massive population? According to traditional Marxist analysis, true proletarian revolution could occur only in an urban, industrial society. In the judgement of Soviet theorists, China, which was a rural and agricultural society, could not be regarded as a fully developed Communist state. Soviet references to the inferiority of the Chinese model aroused the anger of Maoists, who retaliated by accusing the USSR of betraying the cause of world revolution by its pursuit of co-existence with the capitalist West. It was ironic that, although the death of Stalin in 1953 had removed an obvious personal obstacle to better Sino-Soviet relations, Khrushchev's subsequent treatment of the Stalin legend re-awakened Chinese suspicions. His extraordinary assault on Stalin's 'cult of personality' was interpreted in China as a scarcely veiled attack on Mao's own brand of personal leadership.

Despite occasional appearances of understanding, Sino-Soviet relations grew increasingly embittered in the 1950s. Mao acknowledged the special position of the Soviet Union in the history of proletarian struggle, but he made no effort to hide his contempt for what he regarded as Khrushchev's toadying to the West. Mao demanded that the USSR show greater commitment to liberation movements worldwide and abandon 'revisionism', the word for heresy in Marxist vocabulary. In 1957 the Chinese were offered Soviet assistance in developing their own nuclear weapon, but in return Moscow wanted control of Peking's defence policy. The price was too high. Mao rejected the offer, opting instead for a slower but independent Chinese nuclear programme. China was not prepared to play a subordinate role to the USSR.

This became abundantly clear in the following year when Sino-American relations reached breaking point over the USA's military support for Nationalist China in Taiwan, which seemed on the verge of being invaded by Red China. Since taking refuge on Taiwan in 1949, Chiang Kaishek's Nationalists had relied heavily on the USA to prevent Communist China from launching an attack on the island. Such an attack seemed imminent in 1958. In the ensuing crisis Mao expected the USSR to provide Communist China with at least diplomatic, if not military, backing. However, the Soviet Union had no wish to become involved. Khrushchev declared 'the time is not ripe for the socialist world to test the stability of the capitalist system' and refused to make any commitment to the Chinese Communists. To Mao, who did not proceed with the invasion, this was further proof of Khrushchev's betrayal of the international Communist cause.

These profound disagreements over foreign policy and Marxist ideology were deepened by disputes over territory. In the late 1950s and 1960s, the USSR and China stationed large numbers of troops along their joint border in central Asia. Incidents were frequent and threatened to lead to a major confrontation. When a border war between China and India broke out in 1962, the USSR remained officially neutral, but unofficially let it be known that it supported the Indian case. The Sino-Soviet gap widened still further. In the same year, that gap became a gulf as a result of the Cuban missile crisis. China fiercely criticised the Soviet Union on two counts: first, for siting its rockets so clumsily that they were easily detected; second, for its craven submission to the American ultimatum.

1963 marked the lowest point in the relations of the two Communist powers. China refused to join the USA and the USSR in signing the Test-Ban Treaty. Moscow condemned this as proof of Mao's irresponsibility. Khrushchev claimed that Mao wanted to see the old world, capitalist and Communist, engage in mutual nuclear destruction, thus leaving China free to dominate the world that remained. Mao responded by denouncing the Soviet Union for reneging on its revolutionary duty: 'Soviet revisionist collaborators are uniting with the running dogs of capitalism'. The Soviet Union reverted to Russian tradition by talking of the 'yellow peril', the spectre of the vast population of China over-running Europe from the east, with Russia as the first victim. At an ideological level, Mao and his colleagues were branded as 'petty bourgeois, not true proletarian revolutionaries'. Mao retaliated by dismissing the Soviet leaders as 'fascists, unworthy of the Marxist-Leninist inheritance'. These were not gratuitous insults. By describing Khrushchev and the Kremlin as the betrayers of revolution, Mao was encouraging Communists in all other countries to reject the Soviet lead and turn to the Chinese model of Marxism.

There was a markedly personal element in all this. Khrushchev and Mao Zedong had developed a deep distaste for each other. Khrushchev referred to Mao as 'a living corpse', while Mao spoke of the Soviet leader as 'an old boot to be thrown into the corner because it is no longer of any use'. Western observers often found such exchanges comic, but behind the insults was a deadly serious battle for ascendancy in the Communist world. Instead of developing into the great monolith that the West had feared, international Communism had fissured. China and the Soviet Union, the two Marxist giants, were engaged in a bitter competition to win the loyalty and support of the rest of the Communist world. The public squabbling brought Khrushchev little credit and the scandal of Sino-Soviet disharmony was a factor in the weakening of his position within the USSR. At the time of his fall from power in October 1964, which by coincidence was the same month in which China exploded its first atomic bomb, Khrushchev was still trying to rally the Communist world against the Chinese heretics.

8 The Fall of Khrushchev

> **KEY ISSUE** What factors had undermined Khrushchev's
> leadership of the Soviet Union by 1964?

In October 1964 Khrushchev took a holiday at a Black Sea resort.
During his absence from Moscow the Politburo met and decided on
his removal as leader. It is now known from the KGB's archives that
serious consideration was given to having Khrushchev assassinated,
but in the end a milder fate for him was decided on. A meeting of the
Central Committee was convened and Khrushchev was summoned
back to Moscow to appear before it. He was informed that he had
retired through age and poor health and that he had been replaced
by Leonid Brezhnev (who previously had been foremost in suggesting
assassination) and Alexei Kosygin. The news was publicly announced
on the radio and in *Pravda*. The other Moscow newspaper, *Izvestia*,
whose editor was Khrushchev's son-in-law, was not allowed to appear
that day. Accepting that he had been completely outmanoeuvred and
had no allies, Khrushchev slipped away into obscure retirement.
Some days later *Pravda* published a lengthy editorial in which, without referring to him by name, Khrushchev's weaknesses and errors
were listed:

I   The Leninist Party is the enemy of subjectivism, individualism and drift-
    ing in Communist construction, of hare-brained scheme-making, of half-
    baked conclusions and hasty decisions and actions taken without regard
    to realities. Bragging and phrase-mongering, bossiness, reluctance to
5   take account of scientific achievement and practical experience are alien
    to it.
        It is only on the Leninist principle of collective leadership that it is
    possible to direct and develop the increasing creative initiative of the
    Party.[8]

The manner of Khrushchev's demotion and the substance of *Pravda*'s
criticisms are instructive. Whatever his achievements may have been
in the previous decade, it is clear that by the autumn of 1964 he was
politically friendless and isolated. However necessary de-Stalinisation
may have been, Khrushchev in introducing it had provided the
grounds for his own eventual dismissal. The attack upon 'the cult of
personality' created the language and the precedent for removing
any subsequent leader whose personal authority grew too large. In
Stalin's time, his subordinates were too frightened to oppose him.
This had never been so with Khrushchev. He had had to overcome
challenges in the 1950s, and the reason that there was no organised
move against him until 1964 is to be explained by a lack of opportunity rather than by a lack of will. All Stalin's colleagues had owed
their positions directly to his patronage. Khrushchev never wielded

that same authority. It is true that some of the middle and lower rank officials were his protégés, but he never had the control of the Party and governmental machine that Stalin had possessed.

The members of the collective leadership that succeeded Stalin owed nothing to Khrushchev for the positions they held. Even in his best years as leader, Khrushchev was ultimately answerable to the Politburo and Central Committee whose members were individually his political equals and collectively his master. Of course, in any political system strength of personality counts for a good deal. In the earlier years of his leadership, Khrushchev's gregarious style and jocularity made a welcome change from the grim joylessness of Stalin. But these attributes were of advantage only when things were going well for him. As the *Pravda* editorial made clear, when his reputation began to wane his style and manner were characterised as personal failings.

Khrushchev was a highly industrious and very visible leader of the Soviet Union. He took a direct part in a wide range of domestic and foreign affairs. This close personal involvement had its obvious advantages, but it also made him vulnerable. When policies failed, he appeared responsible in a way that a less energetic leader would not have been. There was no single event that caused his fall into disfavour. It was rather that as time went on his policy failures tended to outweigh his successes. Dissatisfaction accumulated. In retrospect, it is possible to identify those areas of growing opposition and to determine why, by 1964, he had no significant political support on which he could rely.

Khrushchev's attempts to streamline and decentralise many areas of Party and government involved him in a continuous struggle with the forces of Soviet bureaucracy. Stalinism had been a heavily bureaucratic system. The Communist Party under Stalin had been the great dispenser of jobs and patronage. When Khrushchev sought to rationalise the system and make it more effective he challenged the livelihood of a whole army of officials and functionaries. They were not likely to regret his political demotion.

A more far-reaching challenge to the old ways had been Khrushchev's de-Stalinisation initiative. This had been a calculated risk. He was aware of how ingrained Stalinism was in the USSR. After decades of Stalin-worship, it was a huge psychological wrench for Party members to admit that the great leader had been so wrong on so many counts. Some of the old guard, such as Molotov and Kaganovich, could not bring themselves to accept the total destruction of the Stalin legend. For the sake of expediency, they went along with de-Stalinisation, but they remained fearful of what it might reveal about their own past. They thought also that it threatened the claims and reputation of the Party. Moreover, the greater freedom of expression given to writers and artists in the post-Stalin 'thaw' seemed to them to be an added and unnecessary danger. The Party die-hards did not easily forgive Khrushchev for placing such hazards in the path of traditional Soviet Communism.

In his rise to prominence in the mid-1950s Khrushchev had been able to rely on the considerable backing of the leaders of the armed forces, but by 1964 that support had been largely forfeited. This was mainly the result of his wish to cut or redirect military expenditure. By the mid-1950s the USSR could genuinely be defined as a super-power: it possessed the H-bomb and was making significant advances in missile development. Khrushchev felt that this justified a cut-back in conventional forces. In 1960 he proposed reducing the armed services by over a million men, a cut of one-third. Such developments, taken together with the loss of Soviet military prestige over Cuba, meant that by 1964 he had exhausted the goodwill of the generals.

In foreign affairs, to which he had devoted so much of his energy, Khrushchev suffered a similar decline in his fortunes. In personal terms there was no doubt that he had become a truly international statesman; his foreign travels and summit diplomacy were unprecedented in Soviet tradition. Despite this, there were few successes to which he could point. He had entered into a long and unresolved conflict with China to retain the moral leadership of the USSR in the Communist world. He had awakened hopes of independence in the Eastern-bloc countries, only to dash them by military intervention and the reimposition of Soviet control. He had fought a running Cold War battle with the West over Germany, but had been unable to deliver the peace treaty by which he had set such store. He had then dismayed the East Germans by his overtures to Bonn. Almost as a last throw he had tried to recover his diplomatic losses by the installation of Soviet missiles in Cuba, only to have to back down in the face of American determination. These undeniable failures aroused bitterness in his Kremlin colleagues.

Arguably, the severest measure by which leaders are judged, whether in capitalist or Communist countries, is the economic one. Khrushchev had promised a more productive Soviet economy, geared to the interests of the consumer but still capable of overhauling the West. It was a brave but unrealistic boast. Advances were made, but the basic problems inherited from Stalin were still there in the mid-1960s. Ironically, his most far-sighted policy, the reclamation of the virgin lands, was the one which, in his own time, brought him the greatest criticism and discredit.

Those involved in the plot to oust him in 1964 could be confident that the range of Soviet interests angered or disillusioned by Khrushchev's policies during the previous eight years was such that there would be little resistance to his removal. The view of one of his Soviet contemporaries provides a fitting insider's assessment of Khrushchev's basic weakness:

1 It is normal for a leader to be feared or cursed or criticized, but when he is laughed at and made the butt of jokes, his time is up. After the sinister giants Lenin and Stalin, it seems that in the end Khrushchev was somehow too lightweight a figure for the public … As a reformer he
5 was not understood, while many were simply not willing to forgive him for exposing the personality cult.[9]

References

1 In Dmitri Volkogonov, *The Rise and Fall of the Soviet Empire: Political Leaders from Lenin to Gorbachev* (HarperCollins, 1998), p.183.
2 In Bertram D. Wolfe, *Khrushchev and Stalin's Ghost* (Frederick A. Praeger, 1957), pp.140–46.
3 *Ibid.*, pp.200–02
4 Note from the Government of the USSR to the Government of the USA, 18 October 1955.
5 Note from the Government of the USSR to the Governments of France, Great Britain and the USA, 27 November 1958.
6 Dmitri Volkogonov, *The Rise and Fall of the Soviet Empire: Political leaders from Lenin to Gorbachev* (HarperCollins, 1998) p.238.
7 *Ibid.*, p.247.
8 *Pravda*, 28 October 1964.
9 In Dmitri Volkogonov, *The Rise and Fall of the Soviet Empire*, p.247.

Summary
'Khrushchev'

The Stalin Legacy

Bureaucracy	Cult of Personality	Economic Imbalance	The Cold War

De-Stalinisation

Streamlining	Party Control	Decentralisation	Co-existence

Khrushchev's fall

Bureaucracy Reacts	Cult of Personality	Virgin-lands Policy	Germany Cuba China

Working on Chapter 6

There are five key themes to concentrate on: Khrushchev's rise, his policy of de-Stalinisation, his economic reforms, his foreign policy, and his fall. If you take a comparative approach, contrasting Khrushchev's policies with those of Stalin, you will provide yourself with an effective basis on which to build your understanding of all five areas. Use the Key Issues to guide you in this.

Answering structured and essay questions on Chapter 6

1. a) Describe the steps taken by Khrushchev to achieve power in the USSR by 1956.
   b) Why had the collective leadership that followed Stalin broken down by 1956?
2. a) Outline the main points made by Khrushchev in his 'secret speech' in 1956.
   b) Explain why Khrushchev chose to embark on a policy of de-Stalinisation.
3. a) Describe the essential features of Khrushchev's industrial strategy.
   b) How far do you agree with the view that Khrushchev's 'virgin lands' policy was 'a success concealed within a failure'?
4. a) In what ways did Khrushchev attempt to improve the Soviet Union's relations with the West in the period 1956-64?
   b) Explain why Khrushchev pursued a policy of co-existence with the Western powers.
5. a) Describe the main features of the German problem that Khrushchev inherited.
   b) How close do you consider Khrushchev came to satisfactorily resolving the German problem?
6. a) Trace the steps by which the Soviet Union came to install nuclear weapons on the island of Cuba in 1962.
   b) How serious a diplomatic defeat for the Soviet Union was the eventual settlement of the Cuban missile crisis?
7. a) Describe the basic issues dividing the USSR and the People's Republic of China in the period between the death of Stalin and the fall of Khrushchev.
   b) 'Sino-Soviet hostility resulted not from a conflict of national interests but from a clash of personalities at the top.' How far do agree with this view?
8. a) Describe the main areas of opposition to Khrushchev that had arisen within the Soviet Union by 1964.
   b) 'Khrushchev fell from power in 1964 because he had tried to do too much, too soon'. How far do agree with this view?

Consider Questions 8b. Obviously, you need to address the quotation directly by describing what Khrushchev attempted to do. Draw on your knowledge of his domestic and foreign policy initiatives to establish this. You will then be in a position to begin judging the 'too much, too soon' aspects. The question of the volume and the speed of his attempted reforms points you to the nature of the problems confronting Khrushchev in the post-Stalin era. The Stalin legacy, the inertia of the bureaucracy and the resistance of Soviet vested interests to change meant that Khrushchev faced great obstacles. Ask yourself whether he tackled these in the most effective way. Were there genuine alternatives? Did he have the necessary time? Try to link your points together, so that they provide a coherent response to the question.

7 The Soviet Record, 1924–64

POINTS TO CONSIDER

In Chapter 1 it was suggested that the problems of Revolutionary Russia in the 40 years between the death of Lenin and the fall of Khrushchev could be expressed in three questions relating to the power structure, the economy and foreign relations. The present chapter follows this pattern by assessing the record of Stalin and Khrushchev in relation to these three questions.

1 The Exercise of Power

KEY ISSUE How was power exercised in the Soviet state?

It is one of the many paradoxes of Soviet history that the Communist movement, which in theory drew its authority from the will of the masses, became so dependent on the idea of the great leader. It was the memory of Lenin's dominance of the Bolshevik Party that endured as the most powerful legacy of the 1917 Revolution. Lenin's practical skills had been necessary to put Marx's ideas into effect. After 1917 reverence for the achievements of Lenin became a vital part of Communist tradition. It was Stalin's ability to suggest that he was continuing the work of Lenin that eased his own path to supremacy in the USSR after 1924. Circumstances had made loyalty to the Party and loyalty to Lenin inseparable. Similarly, by the late 1920s Stalin had succeeded in identifying his own authority with that of the rule of the Party. This made it extremely difficult for his fellow Communists to oppose him. To criticise Stalin was equivalent to doubting Lenin, the Party and the Revolution.

Stalin's intimate knowledge of the workings of the Secretariat aided him in his rise to power. By 1924 he had come to hold a number of important administrative positions, chief of which was the office of General Secretary of the CPSU. This left him ideally placed to control the appointment of members to the various posts within the Party's gift. Stalin became the indispensable link-man in the expanding system of Soviet government. Large numbers of Communist officials owed their positions to Stalin's influence. They could not afford to be disloyal to him. This gave him a power-base which his rivals could not match. In the 1920s he was able to defeat all other contenders in the power struggle that followed Lenin's death. The clear proof of how powerful Stalin had become was evident in the 1930s when he launched a series of purges of his real or imagined enemies in the government, the armed services and the

Party. From then until his death in 1953, he exercised absolute authority over the Soviet Union.

An argument once raged among scholars over whether the totalitarianism of Stalin was a logical progression from the authoritarianism of Lenin, or whether it was the responsibility of Stalin alone. Isaac Deutscher and Roy Medvedev, both of whom suffered under Stalin, followed Trotsky in suggesting that Stalin had perverted the basically democratic nature of Leninism into a personal dictatorship. However, Alexander Solzhenitsyn, a leading dissident Soviet writer who underwent long years of imprisonment in the gulag, regarded Stalin as a 'blind, mechanical executor of Lenin's will' and stressed that the apparatus of the police state was already in place when Stalin took over. One-party rule, the secret police, the use of terror tactics, show trials: these were already in existence by 1924. Solzhenitsyn's analysis was backed by Western commentators such as Edward Crankshaw and Robert Conquest, who described Stalin's tyranny as simply a fully developed form of Lenin's essentially repressive creed of revolution.

The views of such writers were given powerful support by the opening up of the Soviet state archives in the 1990s following the fall of Communism and the break-up of the USSR. Robert Service, in his authoritative study of Lenin, published in 2000, pointed to an essential link between Lenin and Stalin. He produced compelling evidence to establish his claim that Stalin, far from corrupting Lenin's policies, had fulfilled them. He confirmed that all the main features of the tyranny that Stalin exerted over the Soviet State had been inherited directly from Lenin.

Dmitri Volkogonov, the Russian biographer of the great trio who made the Russian revolution, Lenin and Stalin and Trotsky, went further. In his study of the seven men who led Soviet Russia between 1917 and 1991, he suggested that not only was there a direct line of continuity between Lenin and Stalin but that from the first leader, Lenin, to the last, Gorbachev, all shared the same absolutism. While they may have differed as individuals in character and style, they were all united by a belief in the utter correctness of Communism and in the right of the CPSU to dictate to the people of the Soviet Union and to the Socialist world. Though some sought change, none of the seven was a genuine reformer. They could not afford to be since, in the end, to admit that reform was necessary was to admit that Communism could go wrong. Such an admission would have cut the ground from under their feet and made nonsense of all that the Soviet Union claimed to represent. Volkogonov concluded:

1   The one-dimensional approach laid down by Lenin doomed Stalinism
    historically. Created as the theory and practice of 'Lenin's precepts',
    Stalinism from its inception was hidebound by ossified dogmatism. By
    welding the Party organisation to that of the state, Stalinism gradually
5   reshaped the legions of 'revolutionaries' into an army of bureaucrats. By

adopting revolutionary methods to speed up the natural course of events, Stalinism ultimately brought the country to real backwardness.[1]

It is tempting to see the Khrushchev years, coming as they did after the deadly tyranny of Stalin, as a period of liberalism. Certainly, the outgoing Khrushchev presented a sharp personal contrast to the paranoid Stalin who rarely left the Kremlin. However, despite his apparent playfulness and levity, Khrushchev was a resolute upholder of Communist rule in the USSR and its satellites. He was not a libertarian in any Western sense. He wanted to rid the Soviet system of its many bureaucratic encumbrances but he did not want an open society. The USSR under Khrushchev remained totalitarian in all essentials. It remained a one-party state dominated by the CPSU.

In his plans for modernising the Soviet Union, Khrushchev made the momentous decision to destroy Stalin's reputation and change his policies. In doing this he was seeking to reverse 30 years of Soviet history. This was an enormous task that in the end proved too much for him. Khrushchev lost power in 1964 with his objectives largely unfulfilled. The Soviet economy was still under-productive, Soviet standards of living still lagged a long way behind the West, and the USSR was still burdened with a huge defence budget. The irony was that for Khrushchev to undo the work of Stalin he would have had to be another Stalin, but he was never able to exercise that degree of power. Throughout his eight years as Soviet leader, Khrushchev struggled continuously to maintain his authority over Party and government. His removal from office by the united opposition of his Party colleagues was clear proof that he had not been able to control the political machine as Stalin had done.

One of Stalin's enduring legacies was the resistance of those entrenched in the system created by him to the idea of major change in the Soviet Union. It was not so much that Khrushchev's policies were in themselves defective as that he tried to do too much, too soon. He faced formidable opposition from those who, having escaped being purged, came to benefit from Stalinism. The Party, the bureaucracy and the armed services were the chief beneficiaries and, therefore, the guardians of the system Stalin had bequeathed. In attempting to redirect the Soviet Union, Khrushchev was challenging a whole range of vested interests. It was these interests, the forces of Soviet conservatism, that finally defeated him. Volkogonov's reflection is again a telling one:

1 For all his originality, courage and desire for innovation, Khrushchev was a child of his times, and decades of working under Stalin could not but have an effect. He had the manners of a totalitarian dictator: peremptory, arbitrary, concerned with appearances, and harsh when 5 the need arose. He correctly diagnosed the desperate need for deep reform of the economy, but was prepared to alter only the form of administration and management, barely touching its essential nature.

The dictatorial style and previous practice continued, whereby the orders of the leader were not to be questioned. Khrushchev believed
10 it was his right to demote any official who displeased him for whatever reason, and to do so without consultation. He had correctly judged the mood of the moment, which called for reforms, but he tried to carry them out by the old bureaucratic methods.[2]

2 The Economy

> **KEY ISSUE** How did the economy develop under Soviet Communism?

Although historians broadly agree that the industrial revolution enforced on the USSR between 1928 and 1941 was a prodigious achievement, they continue to ask whether it was necessary. Their debate revolves around two essential questions. Did Stalin's industrial programme meet Russia's real economic needs, and was there no alternative to the brutal methods used to accomplish it? With hindsight it is clear that Stalin's economic strategy was based on a distorted view of Western industrialisation and was, therefore, fatally flawed. Stalin misinterpreted the economic difficulties experienced by the Western economies between the two World Wars. It was true that the West underwent a period of relative decline but this proved temporary and this was largely confined to the old-fashioned staple industries of iron, steel, and heavy-goods production, the very areas which Stalin chose to develop in the Soviet Union. The Western world recovered by an expansion of light engineering and modern technology, linked directly to deliberately-stimulated consumer demand.

Stalin turned his back on consumer goods. Under him, Soviet growth was to be in the spectacular areas of steel-mills, oil-refineries, hydro-electric plants, tractor factories and the like. These were the symbols of State power. No concessions were to be made in the USSR to the decadent demands of capitalist-inspired consumerism. In a collectivist State the economy had to serve collective ends, not those of the individual. Such reasoning fitted Communist ideology and it clearly expressed Stalin's perception of the immediate requirements of a Soviet State besieged in a hostile world. But it ran counter to economic reality.

Time would show that Soviet industrialisation, as established by Stalin, would not answer the USSR's long-term needs. Impressive though it was in its short-term gains, Stalin's economic revolution committed the Soviet Union to a form of development that made it impossible for it to realise the main objective of catching up with the world's advanced nations. At the very time when the West, through the bitter experience of the Depression, began to realise the need to abandon its reliance on the traditional heavy industries, Stalin's Russia adopted them as the basis for its own economic future. The result was an unbalanced economy, with over-production of non-essentials and under-production of vital commodities. These problems, compounded by the Soviet Union's chronic food-shortage, were to outlive Stalin and to confront Khrushchev and his successors.

Stalin's methods, the enforcement of collectivisation and industrialisation, are equally controversial. Some observers, then and since, have argued that the special history and character of Russia required a Stalin to effect the necessary transformation of society. Their assertion is that, without an individual of Stalin's authority to lead the way, the Russian people could not have been mobilised on the scale demanded by modernisation. Individual leadership has been the most consistent and powerful political tradition in Russian history. 1917 did not change this. The autocracy of the tsars was simply replaced by the autocracy of Lenin, and then of Stalin. Stalin's popularity among the governing elite came from the perception of him as the leader strong enough to put those ever-troublesome peasants in their place and resolute enough to guide the nation to modernity through the birth pangs of industrialisation.

With this line of reasoning, it is even possible to justify the hardships imposed on the Soviet people. Historical comparisons can be made to show that no society has undergone industrialisation without witnessing disturbance and distress. If the Russian experience appears more painful than most, the explanation lies in the speed and intensity of the changes. A strong argument is that the sufferings of the Russian people under Stalin become historically acceptable when it is remembered that without the enforced industrialisation of the 1930s the Soviet Union could not have sustained itself during the four years of total war from 1941 to 1945. E.H. Carr suggests that without Stalin's 'planned economy' the USSR would have collapsed in wartime.

Those historians who are unmoved by this defence of Stalin's methods have pointed out that, notwithstanding Stalin's claims to be building a war economy, when war did come the USSR was not in fact ready. It was luck not planning that saved the day for Stalin. Furthermore, for all its apparent achievement of Stalin's industrial goals, the Russian economy could not have expanded at the rate that it did had not a sound basis for growth already existed. Writers such as Leonard Shapiro have contended that had the industrial growth under the tsars continued uninterrupted beyond 1914 it would have reached no less a level of expansion by 1941 than that achieved by Stalin's terror strategy. Norman Stone has supported this projection by arguing that without the expertise and basic industrial structures that already existed the Five-Year Plans would have been unable to reach the level of success that they did. Robert Conquest, an especially sharp critic of Stalin's totalitarianism, has remarked:

'Stalinism is one way of attaining industrialisation, just as cannibalism is one way of attaining a high protein diet'.

Those who assert that Stalin's economic policies were mistaken point to the statistics showing that the living standards of Soviet factory-workers in 1953 were barely higher than in 1928, while those of farm-workers were actually lower than in 1913. Khrushchev attempted to redress the imbalance. He opted for decentralised planning, industrial diversification and the encouragement of progressive techniques in agriculture. Unfortunately for him, his measures were soundly conceived but poorly applied. In the relatively short period during which he was leader Khrushchev was unable to change the basic character of the Soviet economy.

At the time, Khrushchev received a bad press at home and abroad for the seeming failure of his agricultural policies. This was largely undeserved. He was struggling to put right in a few years the neglect of a quarter of a century. Stalin's subordination of agriculture to the needs of industry had deprived the land of investment and resources. His collectivisation programme had so disrupted rural life that it would take generations to recover. Khrushchev's reforms were basically sound but he was facing a task that was beyond the means at his disposal. The re-introduction of incentives and the attempt to bring waste-land into production were policies that needed time to develop before they could begin to show returns. It was a problem that beset agricultural reformers in tsarist days as well as in revolutionary Russia. Time was the one thing they were never allowed.

3 Foreign Relations

> **KEY ISSUE** What form did the Soviet Union's foreign policy take?

Stalin's initial approach to foreign policy was expressed in the slogan 'socialism in one country'. He chose to concentrate on the task of securing the revolution in the USSR, regardless of what was happening to the Communist cause elsewhere. His perception of Russia's weakness led him to believe that this was the only policy available. The same perception underlay his decision to enforce industrialisation on the Soviet Union; unless this were undertaken he believed the capitalist West would move to destroy the Soviet Union: 'Either we do it, or we shall be crushed.' International revolution was to be suspended indefinitely until the USSR had consolidated its own position beyond challenge. This was in direct conflict with the revolutionary internationalism of his great Bolshevik rival, Trotsky.

Soviet foreign policy under Stalin became essentially a matter of self-protection. A complication in this respect was that the USSR appeared to speak with two voices. The Comintern, the Moscow-based official mouthpiece of international Communism, continued to talk combatively of the Soviet Union leading the world towards violent revolution. In contrast, the Soviet Foreign Office under Stalin sought to develop diplomatic and commercial contacts with the very states and governments against whom the Comintern was directing its propaganda.

This ambiguity in Soviet attitudes created uncertainty and prevented Stalin and the Soviet Union from ever being fully trusted abroad. It is true that the USSR did enter into a number of commercial agreements in this period but these seldom proved lasting. Moreover, the diplomatic recognition formally accorded the Soviet Union did little to lift the siege atmosphere that prevailed within the country. War scares were a recurrent feature of Soviet life under Stalin. In some respects these suited Stalin's domestic purposes; the threat of invasion made any expression of opposition within Russia appear like treachery. However, they were hardly calculated to present the USSR to foreign observers as a reliable partner with whom they could comfortably do business.

The virulent anti-Bolshevism of Nazi Germany in the 1930s posed a huge threat to the USSR. To nullify this, Stalin attempted first to negotiate defence treaties with France and Britain. When those countries declined to respond, Stalin changed tactics and entered into the Nazi-Soviet non-aggression Pact of August 1939. The security he gained for the USSR by this diplomatic coup proved an illusion. Two years later, Hitler's armies launched their long-prepared invasion and the Soviet Union found itself engaged in a desperate struggle for survival.

The USSR's eventual military victory in 1945 suggested that it was now a world power. Yet, even in triumph, Stalin's defensiveness prevailed. The extraordinary suffering of the Soviet people in the war of 1941-45 became the great formative experience in modern Russian history. The devastation of so much of its territory and the loss of 25 million of its people intensified the Soviet Union's sense of isolation and vulnerability. After 1945, Stalin was even more determined to safeguard his country from any repetition of the foreign occupations that had occurred all too frequently since 1914. The outcome of the war gave him the means of ensuring this. The westward drive of the Soviet armies had left the USSR in control of large areas of Eastern Europe. Stalin now viewed these as buffer zones, guaranteeing Soviet security from the Western powers in general, and Germany in particular. His refusal to release the Soviet grip on these newly acquired regions was a major factor in the development of the Cold War. Equally important in the creation of East-West tension was the issue of nuclear weapons. Stalin had been disturbed by news of the USA's development of an atomic bomb in 1945; he had ordered that, regardless of the economic burden, the necessary resources be granted to Soviet scientists to enable them to produce a comparable weapon. In 1949 this was achieved. The arms-race had begun.

The Cold War, with its iron curtain, its spiralling arms race, and its space rivalry was duly inherited by Khrushchev. He brought a fresh style to Soviet foreign policy. As part of his de-Stalinisation programme he followed a policy of co-existence with the West. Although this new approach was naturally welcomed by Western governments, it has to be seen in Soviet terms. For Khrushchev, co-existence was never simply or primarily a matter of good will. He pursued it because it offered the Soviet Union a way of lightening the heaviest of its economic burdens. The Cold War was colossally expensive. Khrushchev knew that as long as it remained the dominant feature of East-West relations the Soviet Union would be crippled by defence costs, preventing the recovery and expansion of the domestic economy. If it was to honour Khrushchev's repeated pledge to the Soviet people that they would soon overhaul the West, the USSR had to free itself from the shackles of Stalin's restrictive economic policies and adopt modern, expansive programmes. This could not be undertaken as long as international relations remained a matter of confrontation.

Co-existence had its successes, but Khrushchev was faced by mounting problems in foreign relations. The division of Germany and Berlin became increasingly troublesome to the USSR. Encouraged by de-Stalinisation, the Eastern-bloc satellites showed dangerous signs of wanting their independence. China under Mao Zedong began to compete with the Soviet Union for the leadership of the Communist world. Opponents of Khrushchev within the Kremlin used these difficulties to attack his policies. They were provided with still stronger grounds for criticism in 1962; Khrushchev, having taken a Cold War gamble by installing nuclear missiles in Cuba, was forced to withdraw them when confronted by an American ultimatum. Despite his efforts to restructure Soviet foreign policy, Khrushchev left the USSR with as many problems as he had inherited. The pressing question that had confronted the USSR in 1924 – how to guarantee its security in a hostile world? – was still unresolved in 1964.

In his memoirs, written in the late 1960s, Khrushchev claimed that it was as an international statesman that he had made his greatest contribution to the USSR. The claim deserves attention. He had been the first Soviet leader to become widely known outside the USSR, personally representing his country in every continent. He had been one of the first statesmen in any country to develop 'summitry' as a standard form of international diplomacy. He had presided over the USSR's transition into a super-power, triumphantly watching it become a pioneer in space. He had been the first Soviet leader to declare that his country no longer thought in terms of an inevitable armed struggle between the forces of socialism and capitalism, and the first to recognise co-existence as a principle governing the relations between states. These were not inconsiderable achievements.

Yet, during the 40 years since Lenin's death, little appeared to have changed. In 1924, the Soviet Union had been an economically backward, internationally isolated, one-party state. In 1964, at the time of Khrushchev's fall, despite the prodigious effort and suffering of the people in the intervening years, the Soviet economy still lagged behind those of the advanced nations. Although a super-power, in control of Eastern Europe, the Soviet Union was locked in ideological struggle with both West and East. Internally it still remained subject to the rule of an all powerful Communist Party that represented only ten per cent of the people. Despite its revolutionary origins, the Soviet Union in 1964 was a conservative society that remained deeply suspicious of change. This was the enduring legacy of Stalinism.

References

1   Dmitri Volkogonov, *The Rise and Fall of the Soviet Empire: Political Leaders from Lenin to Gorbachev* (HarperCollins, 1998), p.85.
2   Dmitri Volkogonov, *The Rise and Fall of the Soviet Empire: Political Leaders from Lenin to Gorbachev* (HarperCollins, 1998), pp.215–16.

Working on the Chapter 7

This final chapter offers a number of conclusions:

– The method and style of government in Russia between 1924 and 1964 was essentially authoritarian;
– Stalin left a legacy of State and party control that no leader who came after was able to change;
– Stalin's policy of collectivisation was so disruptive that it permanently crippled Soviet agriculture and left the USSR incapable of feeding itself;
– Stalin's policy of enforced industrialisation achieved a remarkable short term success but prevented the USSR from ever developing a modern economy;
– Khrushchev's attempts at reform failed because he challenged the entrenched Soviet bureaucracy which refused to contemplate genuine political or economic change;
– Soviet foreign policy was based on a contradiction. It claimed to be pursuing world Marxist revolution, but invariably put Soviet national interests first and approached all international questions from a defensive position.

To ensure that you have acquired an over-view of the period, test the validity of these propositions by measuring them against your understanding of the earlier chapters of the book, and by asking yourself how far they accord with the viewpoints of the other writers whose work you have studied.

Summary
'The Soviet Record, 1924–64'

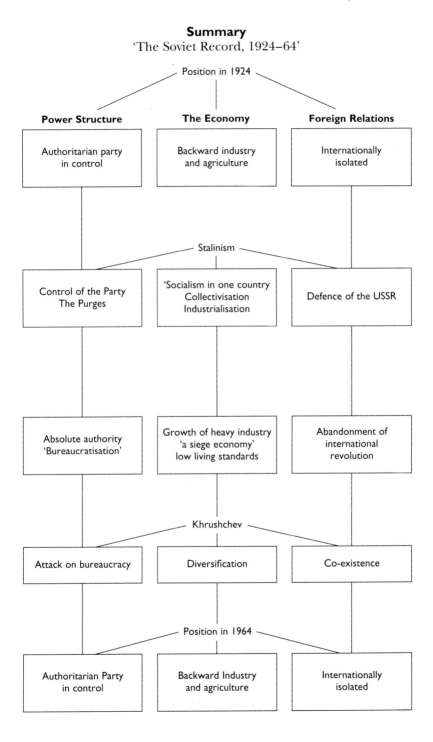

Glossary

Bolshevik The name (meaning 'majority') taken by Lenin and his followers after the split in the SD Party in 1903.

Bourgeoisie The Marxist term for the exploiting capitalist middle class.

CCCP Central Committee of the Communist Party.

Cheka All Russian Extraordinary Commission for Fighting Counter-Revolution (the Bolshevik secret police).

Comintern the Communist International organisation, established in 1919 for the purpose of bringing about revolution in other countries.

Commissar minister or official in the Soviet government or CPSU.

CPSU the Communist Party of the Soviet Union (formerly the Bolshevik Party).

DDR The German Democratic Republic (East Germany)

Glasnost Russian for 'openness', adopted as a description of the new Soviet approach of the late 1980s and 1990s.

Gosplan Superseded *Vesenkha* in 1921 as the body responsible for integrated national economic planning.

Gulag The extensive prison camp system set up under Stalin.

Intelligentsia The educated and more enlightened members of Russian society, who were usually supporters of reform.

KGB The State security force which succeeded the NKVD

Kolkhozy The collective farms.

Konsomol The Young Communist League, a movement for young people between the ages of 14 and 28.

Kulaks The class of rich peasants.

Marxism/Leninism The official Bolshevik/Communist ideology based on the theories of Karl Marx as interpreted by Lenin

Menshevik The word (meaning 'minority') used to describe the followers of Plekhanov after the split in the SD Party in 1903.

MRC The military revolutionary committee of the Petrograd soviet.

NEP The New Economic Policy, introduced by Lenin in 1921, which reintroduced an element of capitalism and relaxed the severe controls imposed on the peasantry

Nepmen The class of merchants and middlemen who profited from the NEP.

NKVD The State security force which succeeded OGPU

OGPU The State security force which succeeded the Cheka

Okhrana (Okhranka) the tsarist secret police.

Orgburo The CCCP's bureau of organisation.

Pogroms Organised persecutions of the Jews.

Politburo The Political Bureau, the inner cabinet of the CCCP.

Pravda Russian for truth, taken as the title of a Bolshevik newspaper, established in 1912.

Proletariat The Marxist term for the revolutionary working class.

Secretariat The CPSU organisation which provided the officials and civil servants who worked for the government

SDs The Social-Democratic Workers' Party which divided into Bolshevik and Menshevik wings in 1903.

Sovkhozy The State collective farms.

Sovnarkom The Council of People's Commissars (the government of the USSR).

USSR The Union of Soviet Socialist Republics, which became the official title of the Soviet state after 1922.

Further Reading

The list of books published on modern Russia grows ever longer, a response to the increasing demand for scholarly information about one of the most remarkable stories in history. The following is a very selective list from the huge number of studies of the Soviet period covered by this book. Where possible, reference is to the latest paperback edition.

1 General Surveys

Authoritative and up-to-date surveys are **Geoffrey Hosking**, *A History of the Soviet Union, Final Edition* (Fontana, 1992), **Robert Service**, *A History of Twentieth-Century Russia* (Allen Lane, 1998), and **Martin Malia**, *The Soviet Tragedy: A History of Socialism in Russia, 1917–1991* (Free Press, 1994). Light on narrative but powerful in analysis is **Walter Laqueur**, *The Dream that Failed: Reflections on the Soviet Union* (OUP, 1994). Thinner in content, but entertainingly written are **Gregory Freeze** *Russia A History* (OUP, 1997) and **Lionel Kochan** and **John Keep**, *The Making of Modern Russia* (Penguin, 1997). A sound text which introduces the key issues is **Michael Kort**, *The Soviet Colossus: History and Aftermath* (M.E.Sharpe, 1996). An older book which retains its value as an introduction is **J.N. Westwood**, *Russia Since 1917* (Batsford, 1980). Students will enjoy the illuminating sections on Russia in **Richard Vinen**, *A History in Fragments: Europe in the Twentieth Century* (Little Brown, 2000). A helpful collection of potted biographies of Soviet personnel is to be found in **Martin McCauley**, *Who's Who in Russian History since 1900* (Routledge, 1997). The same author has also edited a very useful reference book, *The Longman Companion to Russia Since 1914* (Longman, 1998). An outstanding source study of the period, which includes a set of highly informative of linking commentaries, is **Richard Sakwa's** *The Rise and Fall of the Soviet Union, 1917–1991* (Routledge, 1999). Perhaps the most absorbing survey is by the ex-Soviet Communist historian **Dmitri Volkogonov**, who in the 1990s produced a trilogy of biographies on Lenin, Trotsky and Stalin and who just before his death in 1995 completed *The Rise and Fall of the Soviet Empire: Political Leaders from Lenin to Gorbachev* (Harper Collins, 1997).

2 Particular Themes

Students need to appreciate the great importance of economics in the development of Russia in this period. The most accessible study, which begins with an analysis of the economy of imperial Russia, remains **Alec Nove**, *An Economic History of the USSR* (Penguin, 1976).

More difficult but worth persevering with are **R.W. Davies**, (ed.), *The Economic Transformation of the Soviet Union* (CUP, 1994) and **Roger Munting**, *The Economic Development of the USSR*, (Croom Helm, 1982). Soviet social history now receives particular attention from scholars; a leading figure in this field is **Sheila Fitzpatrick**, whose *The Cultural Front: Power and Culture in Revolutionary Russia* (Cornell, 1992) examines the link between political and social developments in Stalinist Russia. An important set of essays on this theme is to be found in **Ian D. Thatcher** (ed), *Regime and Society in Twentieth-Century Russia* (Macmillan, 1999). An informative early work on Stalin's government of the USSR was **Alec Nove**, *Stalinism and After* (Allen and Unwin, 1975). Since the collapse of the USSR and the opening of the Soviet archives, political scientists have joined historians in studying Stalinism as a system of power. Two key texts on this theme are **Robert Tucker** (ed), *Stalinism Essays in Historical Interpretations* (Transaction Publishers, 1999), a collection of essays by leading historians in Russia and the West, and **Sheila Fitzpatrick** (ed), *Stalinism: New Directions* (Routledge, 2000), which gives space to revisionist historians to argue that the Stalinist regime represented a social movement rather than simply the imposition of authority from above. The grim period of collectivisation and the purges has come under intense scrutiny. The best starting point is the work of **Robert Conquest** whose pioneering studies of the effects of famine and repression under Stalin, *The Great Terror: Stalin's Purge of the Thirties* (Penguin, 1971) and, *Harvest of Sorrow* (Macmillan, 1988), were so disturbing that many in the West refused to believe them. However, his findings were confirmed in the harrowing descriptions by the Soviet dissident, **Alexander Solzhenitsyn**, who drew on his own personal experience as a prisoner in Stalin's labour camps in *The Gulag Archipelago* (Collins, 1974–78). Irrefutable proof of Stalin's terror was provided by the archival evidence that came to light during the glasnost years of the late 1980s and after the collapse of the CPSU in the early 1990s. Of the many books that have now studied this theme an outstanding one is **Catherine Merridale**, *Night of Stone: Death and Memory in Russia* (Granta Books, 2000); based on interviews with the survivors of the gulag, it tells the stories of ordinary Russians caught in the grip of Stalinist barbarism. Turning from the suffering of the Soviet people in peacetime to their privations in wartime brings one to **Antony Beevor**, *Stalingrad* (Penguin, 1999); his riveting, if gruesome, book has quickly established itself as a modern classic of military history. On the broader theme of Soviet foreign policy, two highly recommended studies are **Caroline Kennedy-Pipe**, *Russia and the World* (Arnold, 1998), and **Dominic Lieven**, *Empire The Russian Empire and its Rivals* (John Murray, 2000). Those who love spy stories – real ones – will enjoy **Christopher Andrew** and **Vasili Mitrokhin**, *The Mitrokhin Archive: The KGB in Europe and the West* (Penguin, 2000), which tells from the inside the extraordinary tale of Soviet espionage. The remarkable programme of de-Stalinisation undertaken by Khrushchev is still best studied by reference to **Bertram D. Wolfe**, *Khrushchev and Stalin's Ghost* (Frederick A. Praeger, 1957). The importance of the book can be gauged from its subtitle 'Text, Background and Meaning of Khrushchev's Secret Report to the Twentieth Congress on the Night of February 24–25 1956'.

3 Biographies

To understand Stalin it is first necessary to understand Lenin. **Dmitri Volkogonov's**, *Lenin: Life and Legacy* (Harper Collins, 1994) and **Robert Service's**, *Lenin, A Biography* (Macmillan, 2000), are outstanding works, both being based fully on Soviet archives. Valuable for the same reason is **Richard Pipes**, (ed), *The Unknown Lenin: From the Soviet Archives* (Yale, 1996). Of the flood of books on Stalin two are particularly worth singling out: **Roy Medvedev**, *Let History Judge: the Origins and Consequences of Stalinism*, (OUP, 1989) and **Dmitri Volkogonov**, *Stalin: Triumph and Tragedy* (Weidenfeld and Nicholson, 1991). Both these Russian writers worked under the Stalinist system and both became highly critical of its inhumanity. A particularly important study, based on evidence that became available in the *glasnost* years of the 1980s, is **Walter Laqueur**, *Stalin: The Glasnot Revelations* (Macmillan, 1990). Despite having been treated in Stalin's Russia as a 'non-person', Trotsky has been reinstated by modern historians as a vital figure in Soviet history. A short introductory study, specially written for students, is **Michael Lynch**, *Trotsky the Permanent Revolutionary* (Hodder & Stoughton, 1995), while a long but masterly biography is **Isaac Deutscher**, *Trotsky* (OUP, 3 volumes, 1954–70). **Dmitri Volkogonov's** *Trotsky: the Eternal Revolutionary* (Free Press, 1996) completed his great trilogy of the makers of the Russian Revolution. An interesting comparative study that students will appreciate is **Alan Bullock**, *Hitler and Stalin: Parallel Lives*, (Harper Collins, 1991). Stalin's daughter, **Svetlana Alliluyeva**, provides a fascinating and frightening insight into her father's character in *Twenty letters to a Friend* (Penguin, 1968). A notable study of Khrushchev is **Edward Crankshaw**, *Khrushchev: A Biography* (Sphere, 1968); Crankshaw was one of the first Western historians to see a direct line of descent between Lenin, Stalin and Khrushchev. Further scholarly analyses are provided by **Martin McCauley** (ed), *Khrushchev and Khrushchevism* (Indiana University Press, 1987), and **William. J. Thompson**, *Khrushchev: A Political Life* (St.Martin's Press, 1995). Student would find it rewarding to read Khrushchev's reflections on Stalin's and his own role in Soviet history. His memoirs appear in their English form as: **N.S. Khrushchev**, *Khrushchev Remembers* (Andre Deutsch, 1971).

Index